SPEAK
SAFE

LEAD WITH CARE

LEADERSHIP COACHING FROM LEADERSHIP SPECIALIST

ANTON GUINEA

First published by The Rural Publishing Company.

eBook: 978-1-923008-39-7
Print: 978-1-923008-38-0

The Rural Publishing Company
Email: hello@theruralpublishingcompany.com.au
Website: https://theruralpublishingcompany.com.au

SPEAK
SAFE

COMMUNICATION

ACCEPTANCE

RESPONSIBILITY

EMPATHY

CONTENTS

INTRODUCTION

WHY PSYCHOLOGICAL SAFETY IS THE GAME CHANGER

Let's be real for a second.

Psychological safety might sound like one of those fluffy HR buzzwords that gets thrown around in corporate town halls or splashed across a PowerPoint slide – but when you get under the hood of it, it's actually the engine of every high-performing team I've ever worked with.

And every dysfunctional one I've coached? It was the lack of it that was killing the vibe, the results, or both.

Psychological safety isn't about being nice. It's not about holding hands and singing kumbaya at stand-up meetings. It's about creating an environment where people feel safe enough to speak up. To ask questions. To disagree. To own mistakes. To bring forward ideas. And to be *human*.

It's what Harvard professor **Amy Edmondson** defined as 'a belief that one will not be punished or humiliated for speaking up with ideas, questions, concerns, or mistakes.' Sounds simple. It's not. It takes work. It takes leadership. It takes care factor.

That idea? It helped avert a seven-figure failure.

That's psychological safety in action. It's not theoretical. It's transformational.

This book is a playbook. A field manual. A real-talk guide to building safety on your team – one conversation, one decision, and one moment at a time.

Since 2020, when I started recording my coaching sessions, I have completed over 1,350 one-on-one coaching session with leaders for a range of industries, at all levels, in a range of professions.

This book will talk you through what I have learned during those coaching conversations, as well as what I have learnt studying Human Resource and Psychology, amongst other certificates and qualifications.

This book won't reference any studies or research reports. That is deliberate. I want this book to be a real world example of leadership skills, packed with word tracks or conversation tips and tricks that will help you be the leader you want to be.

A psychologically safe leader.

I will bring you some amazing authors and books that you should read, and that will further improve your leadership.

In this book, you'll hear stories – some real, some fictionalised but true to life. You'll get practical tools and prompts to reflect on your leadership. And you'll hear me in your head a little bit, nudging you to lean in and lead with heart.

Because when you speak safe, your people grow. Your team grows. You grow.

Let's get into it.

SECTION 1:

COMMUNICATION

COMMUNICATION

If psychological safety is the house, then communication is the foundation that holds it together as you build.

Every message you send – verbally or non-verbally – is doing one of two things:

- it's re-enforcing psychological safety
- or it is triggering fear.

There is no neutral.

That's why communication sits at the front of this book. It's the gateway. The moment of truth. The daily, minute-by-minute choice to create clarity or confusion, connection or control, safety or silence.

> 'As a leader, your words are tools. And like any tool, they can build – or break the moment, or the relationship.'

What You **SAY**
MATTERS

CHAPTER 1: WHAT YOU SAY MATTERS

You can't not communicate.

That's one of the first things I say when I'm running a leadership program. And when I say it, I always pause. I wait for the confused looks. Then I explain.

Because it's true: even when you're silent, you're sending a message.

Your tone, your body language, your timing, your posture – everything communicates. And in leadership, those micro-messages add up. They either build trust or break it. They either create space for your team to speak up, or they send a subtle warning: stay silent.

And here's the thing – most leaders don't realise they're shutting people down. Not intentionally. Not maliciously. But they do. With just a few words. Or a lack of them.

Let's unpack what that really looks like in the wild.

The Pre-Start Meeting That Shut People Down

It was 6:58 AM. The sun was rising, and the work crew was gathering for their pre-start. Mugs of steaming instant coffee in hand. Steel-cap boots. Hi-vis uniforms. The usual Monday morning mood – tired, half-awake, quietly bracing for the day. Then the supervisor walked in.

He opened with this:

'Righto, let's get this over with – I know everyone's flat out.'

Now, let me be crystal clear – he wasn't trying to be rude. In his mind, he was being respectful of people's time. Efficient. Straight to business.

BUT HERE'S WHAT THE TEAM ACTUALLY HEARD:

- 'Your input doesn't matter'
- 'This is a box-ticking exercise'
- 'Don't speak unless spoken to'

And that's exactly what they did – nothing. No updates. No questions. No heads raised when he asked if there were any concerns.

That same team had flagged a faulty lifting mechanism the previous week but kept quiet that morning. The result? A near miss later that day.

Now here's what happens when you flip the script. Same team. Same time. New leader.

She starts the pre-start by saying:
'Morning, legends. Thanks for making the time this morning – I know Mondays can be a grind. Quick check-in before we dive into the tasks – any wins or worries from last week?'

That tiny shift in words made a massive difference.

Someone shared a small safety concern. Another team member mentioned a supply issue. A third said, 'Hey, can we try a different setup on the scaffolding today? It's been awkward climbing down.' Boom. The team was talking. Contributing. Owning their space.

And it started with one thing: *what was said.*

Words Create Culture

You've probably heard this quote:

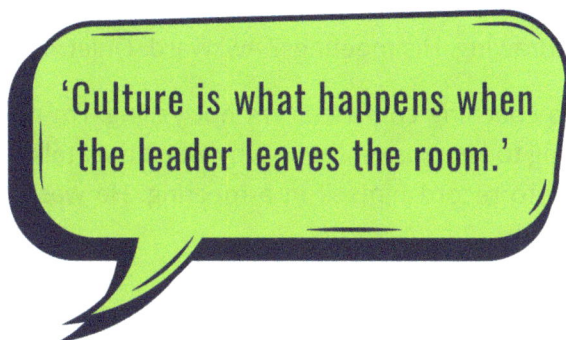

'Culture is what happens when the leader leaves the room.'

I'll take it a step further – language is how that culture is created.

Amy Edmondson, who pioneered the concept of psychological safety, discovered that teams with high safety don't avoid mistakes – they talk about them. They analyse them. They learn from them.

But for that to happen, leaders need to model the behaviour. And the way they do that? Through what they say.

Same goes for **Timothy R. Clark's** '*4 Stages of Psychological Safety*' – leaders build trust by acknowledging people first, then giving them space to contribute, and eventually, challenge the status quo.

You don't get that progression by accident. You get it through intentional language.

Leadership Language in Action

Let me give you a few more examples from the field. These are all fictionalised, but they're based on real coaching situations I've worked through.

Case Study: The Silent Project Manager

'Mike' was a brilliant engineer. When he stepped into a project manager role, he was focused, detailed and organised. But his team? Withdrawing. His meetings? Awkward. Quiet. Tense.

He came to coaching confused. 'I'm not yelling. I'm not blaming. I'm just trying to keep us on track. Why won't they talk to me?' I asked him to record himself in a meeting. He was stunned by what he heard.

HIS GO-TO PHRASES WERE:
- 'Let's just stick to the schedule'
- 'That's already been decided'
- 'I've got it covered'

He thought he was being efficient. What he was actually doing was cutting people off. Every time someone tried to contribute, they were brushed aside. Not aggressively. Just quietly. Repeatedly.

WE WORKED ON SWAPPING IN NEW PHRASES:
- 'Let's pause on that – can you walk me through your thinking?'
- 'Interesting. Tell me more about what you're seeing!'
- 'Is there anything we're missing here?'

After three weeks, his team was buzzing again. He didn't need a new process – he needed a new script.

The Speak Safe Toolkit: Language That Builds Safety

Here's a list of go-to phrases I've given to dozens of leaders who wanted to lift psychological safety in their teams. These work. Use them. Make them your own.

To Invite Input:

- 'I'd love to hear your view on this.'
- 'What do you think we haven't considered?'
- 'I know this might be tricky to bring up, but I'm open to hearing it.'

To Acknowledge Courage:

- 'Thanks for raising that. That takes guts.'
- 'I really appreciate you calling that out.'
- 'That's a hard truth, and I'm grateful for it.'

To Respond to Mistakes:

- 'Thanks for being upfront – let's talk about what we learned.'
- 'That didn't go to plan, but I'm glad we're talking about it.'
- 'What could we do differently next time?'

To Show You're Listening:

- 'Can I repeat that back to make sure I got it?'
- 'That makes sense. Tell me more.'
- 'Hmm. I hadn't thought of it that way before.'

To De-escalate During Tension:

- 'Let's slow it down for a second.'
- 'I can see this matters – let's work through it together.'
- 'Let's assume positive intent and dig in.'

These aren't scripts to read line by line. They're mindset markers. They signal to your team: This is a safe space to speak up.

What Happens When You Get It Wrong

I want to be honest – there will be moments where you say the wrong thing. Where your tone's off. Where you react instead of respond. That's part of being human.

But here's the difference between leaders who build safety and those who destroy it: the good ones *own it.*

I once watched a leader completely misread a comment in a team meeting and snap back at their team member.

They caught themselves, paused, and said:

'Hang on. That came out wrong. I'm under pressure today, but that's no excuse. I appreciate what you said, and I want to understand more. Can we go back a step?'

That moment – *that humility* – repaired what could have been weeks of damage.

Your words matter. But so does how you recover from them.

LEADER REFLECTION AND ACTIVITIES
PROMPT 1: LEADERSHIP LANGUAGE AUDIT

Over the next week, notice three things:

What's your default opening line in meetings?

What's your most common phrase when someone disagrees with you?

How do you respond when someone gives you bad news?

Write down the actual words you use. Then ask:

Are they creating safety, or killing it?

What could I replace them with?

PROMPT 2: 'BEFORE YOU SPEAK' FILTER

Before your next leadership conversation, try this:

- ✅ Ask: What message do I want this person to walk away with?

- ✅ Ask: How do I want them to feel when this ends?

- ✅ Then build your language backwards from there

MINI-PRACTICE: POSITIVE INTERRUPTIONS

In your next team meeting, make a point to interrupt someone positively. For example:

- o 'Hey, before we move on – I just want to highlight what Sam just said.'
- o 'Can we pause there? That idea deserves a bit more airtime.'

That kind of moment shows your team:
We notice. We listen. We care.

COACH'S WRAP-UP

Leadership isn't about titles or task lists – it's about trust. And trust is built one word at a time.

The best leaders I've coached weren't always the smartest in the room. But they were the most intentional. They chose words that lifted people, not language that crushed them.

Your voice is your leadership signature. Use it well.
Speak with clarity. Speak with curiosity. Speak safe.
Let's go build something great.

Is it safe to ask

Questions

and make mistakes?

CHAPTER 2: THE DRIVERS OF PSYCHOLOGICAL SAFETY

The Four Stages of Psychological Safety

While psychological safety is often talked about as one thing, the truth is – it develops in stages. Like building trust, it's a layered process, and each layer matters.

Leadership expert **Timothy R. Clark**, author of *The 4 Stages of Psychological Safety*, outlines a progression that teams and individuals move through as safety increases. Understanding these four stages can help you identify where your team is stuck – and what leadership behaviours are needed next.

Let's walk through each stage:

1. INCLUSION SAFETY

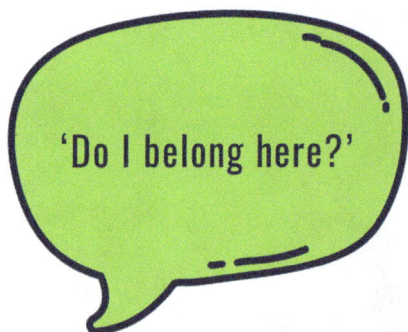

'Do I belong here?'

This is the foundation. People want to know:
Am I accepted for who I am, without needing to conform or hide parts of myself?

If someone feels excluded because of their background, personality, neurodiversity, role, or communication style – psychological safety ends here.

As a leader, you build inclusion safety when you:

- Learn people's names, pronouns, and preferences
- Show consistent respect across roles and ranks
- Invite quieter voices and underrepresented perspectives

Celebrate individuality – not just conformity

Without inclusion, you'll never get honest feedback. People are too busy trying to fit in to speak up.

2. LEARNER SAFETY

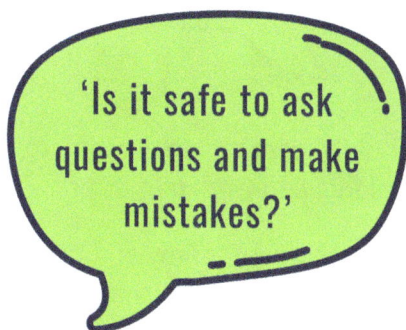

'Is it safe to ask questions and make mistakes?'

Once someone feels they belong, they begin to explore. But exploration brings vulnerability.

If team members are mocked for not knowing something – or punished for making mistakes – they'll shut down, stay silent, and stop growing.

You build learner safety when you:

- Normalise saying 'I don't know'
- Praise effort and curiosity, not just correctness
- Share your own learning edges openly
- Treat mistakes as data – not weakness.

This stage unlocks growth, collaboration, and innovation. Without it, you'll have surface-level engagement – and people playing it safe.

3. CONTRIBUTOR SAFETY

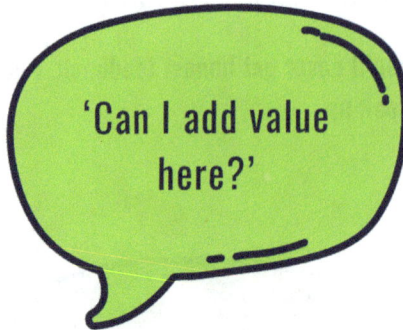

> 'Can I add value here?'

Once people feel safe learning, they want to contribute. They want their ideas, talents and work to matter.

Contributor safety is about autonomy and trust. If every decision is second-guessed or every idea dismissed, safety stalls.

You build contributor safety when you:

- Empower people to lead small projects or ideas
- Give credit publicly
- Create structures for shared problem-solving
- Trust people to deliver – then get out of their way

This stage is where psychological safety gets visible. People speak up. They take initiative. They challenge the status quo. And the work gets better.

4. CHALLENGER SAFETY

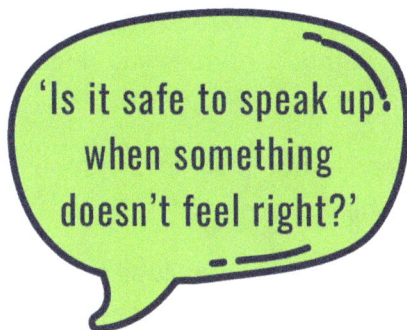

'Is it safe to speak up!
when something
doesn't feel right?'

This is the pinnacle. The bravest kind of safety. It's when someone says:

- 'I think we're missing something.'
- 'This isn't working.'
- 'I disagree – with respect.'

If people are punished, ignored, or sidelined for challenging decisions, they'll revert to silence – even if it means letting bad ideas go unchallenged.

You build challenger safety when you:

- Thank people for dissent, not just agreement
- Create 'challenge channels' in meetings
- Don't shoot the messenger
- Lead with humility: 'What am I not seeing?'

When challenger safety is strong, you don't just prevent errors – you unlock transformation.

Why the Stages Matter

These stages build sequentially. You can't jump to contributor or challenger safety without establishing inclusion and learner safety first.

Psychological safety is not built in a day – it's built in every moment of leadership.

And it's fragile. You might have built all four stages – but it only takes one poor reaction to push someone back down the ladder.

Your job as a leader is to keep moving people forward.

To keep people moving forward, and moving towards creating challenger safety, leaders need to understand the psychological safety drivers.

Let's Get Clear: What Drives Psychological Safety?

Here's a leadership truth bomb: psychological safety doesn't just *happen.*

It's not the result of a great offsite. It's not something you 'achieve' after one good month of check-ins. It's the product of very specific behaviours, repeated consistently, over time.

In my work with teams across mining, energy, government, health – you name it – the high-performing teams all have one thing in common: they've built psychological safety on *purpose.*

And the ones in turmoil? You guessed it. It's not that they don't care. It's that they're not *driving* the right behaviours to build safety.

So, let's unpack it. What drives it? What are the levers you can pull as a leader to make your team feel safe to speak up?

Here's the short answer:

Integrity. Respect. Consistency. Care.

But let's go deeper.

Meet the Team: Fictional Scenario

Let me take you into a fictional team – one inspired by a dozen I've worked with.

This is a team of eight in a regional infrastructure business. Good people. Highly skilled. But fractured.

Why?

- **Two team members don't speak in meetings.**
- **One dominates every conversation.**
- **The team leader – let's call her Brooke – is stressed, stretched, and starting to spiral.**

On paper, this team should fly. But performance is patchy. Culture? Meh. And safety incidents are creeping up. Not the physical ones (yet) – but near misses, mistakes and close calls that no one wants to talk about.

Brooke calls me in. 'Anton,' she says, 'I don't know what else to do. I've been giving them space. I've pulled back. I don't micromanage. But they just don't engage.'

And that's where the light bulb goes on.

Psychological Safety Is Not About Absence

Let's clear this up now: pulling back isn't leadership. Leaving people alone and 'not being the problem' doesn't automatically create safety. Psychological safety is not about absence. It's about presence.

It's about proactive behaviours. Consistent modelling. Open conversation. And a care factor that's visible.

Brooke wasn't damaging her team – but she wasn't developing them either. She was neutral. And neutrality doesn't build safety.

So, we walked through the four core drivers.

Driver 1: Integrity – The Foundation

Integrity is where safety starts. Without it, nothing else works.
But integrity isn't built by big gestures – it's built in micro-moments:

- Following through on what you said you'd do.
- Being honest when you don't know something.
- Backing your team up when they take a risk that doesn't work.

Real Talk Scenario

One of Brooke's team members, Leo, had suggested a process change on the maintenance schedule. Brooke loved it – but her boss didn't.

Later that week, in a senior leadership meeting, her GM asked why the schedule had been altered.

Brooke said:
'It was Leo's idea – we were just trialing it.'

Wrong move.
What Leo heard was: *I'm not protected. If things go wrong, I'm on my own.*

We unpacked this in coaching. Brooke didn't mean to throw Leo under the bus – but that's what it felt like.

Better language:

'I asked Leo to trial an efficiency idea. I stand by the decision to test it – we're learning from it.'

That's what trust sounds like. Own the decision. Protect your team. Build the bridge.

Driver 2: Respect – The Non-Negotiable

If trust is the foundation, respect is the frame.

Respect means every voice matters. Every idea gets airtime. Every person is treated like a professional – even when they're struggling.

Here's something I've noticed in unsafe teams: people talk *about* each other, not to each other. Gossip replaces dialogue. Sarcasm replaces curiosity.

Whenever I get a call from a leader who has a team in turmoil, the first thing that I ask is 'what's the person's name?' I ask this because it is generally only one person in every dysfunctional team that causes the issues for everyone. Note that sometimes it can be two people in a team that are causing issues.

If it is two people then the next question I ask is 'how much gossip is there in the team?' The answer is usually ... a lot.

Gossip is the quickest way to disrespect someone. When team members gossip about each other, your team is doomed to low performance.

When respect is missing, resentment takes over.

Respect is not just about talking about others, it is about giving everyone a voice.

Coaching Insight

Brooke had one team member – Jack – who constantly interrupted others in meetings.

After a few roleplays, I coached Brooke to try this:

'Jack, I really value your input. I also want to make sure everyone gets their say. Let's pause and hear from Nina before we circle back to you.'

That one sentence changed the team dynamic.

Respect isn't about being polite. It's about *prioritising contribution over control*.

Driver 3: Consistency – The Reinforcer

Inconsistent leadership kills safety. Period.

If one week you're approachable, and the next you're reactive, your team doesn't know what version of you they're going to get. That uncertainty? It breeds fear. And fear leads to silence.
Timothy R. Clark said it best:

'If you punish vulnerability, you teach your team to hide it. Consistency tells your team: This is a safe pattern. It's okay to speak. I won't change the rules mid-conversation.'

Fictional Scenario

Brooke had a habit of mood-based leadership. When she was in a good headspace, she'd invite feedback. When she was under pressure? Walls up.

We worked on building 'conscious control' – that skill of showing up consistently, even when things go BOOM.

I had her create a pre-meeting ritual:
- 3 breaths
- A gratitude reminder (what's going right?)
- A safety prompt: 'How can I make this feel safe for them today?'

That tiny routine helped her lead with presence. Predictability. Peace.

And safety followed.

Driver 4: Care Factor – The X-Factor

This one's, my favourite. And it's what I believe *truly* separates good leaders from great ones.

CARE FACTOR IS THE DIFFERENCE BETWEEN:
- 'I'm here to manage you,' and
- 'I'm here to see you succeed.'

YOU CAN'T FAKE CARE. BUT YOU CAN SHOW IT:
- Remember what your team members are working through (at work and home).
- Say 'thank you' more than you think you need to.
- Ask, 'How are you travelling?' and mean it.

Real Example

When one of Brooke's team members had a parent fall ill, we roleplayed how she might check in.

Her first instinct was to say, 'Let me know if you need time off.' Instead, I suggested this:

'I imagine this week's been hard. Do you want to talk through how we can lighten the load for now?'

That one shift – from formality to humanity – meant the world to her team.

And you know what happened? That team member worked harder than ever once they were supported. Because *support builds commitment.*

Measuring the Drivers

You can't manage what you can't measure. So let's make this real. Here's a simple self-diagnostic you can rate yourself on.
1 = never, 5 = always:

Driver	Statement	Score (1–5)
Integrity	I follow through on what I say.	
Respect	I give everyone space to contribute in meetings.	
Consistency	I show up predictably and manage my emotions Under pressure	
Care Factor	I regularly check in on my team as humans, not just workers.	
Total /20		

- **16–20:** You're actively driving safety – keep reinforcing.
- **10–15:** You're on the right track – choose one area to dial up.
- **Below 10:** Time for a reset – pick one driver and start there.

The link to physical safety

This book is focused on psychological safety, and how to have conversations that help leaders have conversations that build high performing teams, through communication that is focused on acceptance, responsibility and empathy.

In high risk organisations, like heavy industries, there is a clear link between physical and psychological safety.

Improving physical safety (aka – sending people home to their families uninjured) takes the same skills from a leader as does increasing psychological safety. The drivers of a safe culture are similar, regardless of whether you are trying to prevent physical or psychological injury.

It is all about safety leadership.

In his ground-breaking work on human-centred safety leadership, **Clive Lloyd** offers a simple but powerful framework for building psychological safety, trust, and care in the workplace.

His model is similar to the CARE model, and spells out what leaders must …

C.R.E.A.T.E.:

C – Care
Do your people believe you genuinely care about them as human beings?
Care isn't just sentiment – it's action. Leaders who care check in, not just check up.

They make time for people, they notice when someone's off, and they lead with compassion – even under pressure.

R – Respect
Do your team members feel seen, heard, and valued?
Respect shows up in the language you use, how you listen, and whether or not you take people seriously. Respect is foundational to trust – and it's a daily leadership choice.

E – Empowerment
Do your people feel they have control, input, and autonomy?
Empowerment means giving your team permission and the tools

to make decisions, raise concerns, and improve how things are done. It's trust in action.

A – Active Listening

Are you truly listening – or just waiting for your turn to speak?
Active listening means putting away distractions, making eye contact, reflecting back what you've heard, and asking deeper questions. It signals: *'You matter, and I want to understand.'*

T – Trust

Do people believe you'll do what you say – and say what you mean?
Trust is the currency of leadership. You earn it through consistent behaviour, honesty (even when it's uncomfortable) and following through on your word.

E – Engagement

Are you present and invested in your people – or just ticking boxes?
Engaged leaders are visible, available, and curious. They walk the floor, join conversations, and make psychological safety a lived value – not just a slogan.

Lloyd's work focuses on safety leadership in high-risk industries, but the lessons are universal: culture shifts when leaders lead from *care, not compliance.*

'It's not enough to manage safety – you have to lead it,' Lloyd says. 'And that starts with human connection.'

The C.R.E.A.T.E. model gives leaders a map – one that moves beyond metrics and policy into meaningful relationships, where people feel safe to speak up, own mistakes, and work together toward something better.

LEADER REFLECTION AND ACTIVITIES

✓ Step 1: Pick one team meeting this week.

✓ Step 2: Choose one driver to focus on during that meeting.

✓ Step 3: Use one of the coaching phrases in real time.

✓ Step 4: After the meeting, reflect:

- How did the team respond?
- What felt different?
- What do I want to try next?

Write your thoughts in your leadership journal. Or better yet – share them with a peer. The best learning is shared.

COACH'S WRAP-UP

Psychological safety isn't just a feeling – it's a *function*. And it's driven by you.

You don't have to be perfect. You just have to be present. Predictable. And human.

Trust is the foundation. Respect is the frame. Consistency is the glue. Care factor is the heartbeat.

When you lead with these four drivers in mind, you're not just building a safer team – you're building a braver one.

One that solves problems faster. One that grows from failure. One that *thrives*.

So let's speak safe, act brave, and drive the behaviours that unlock your team's potential.

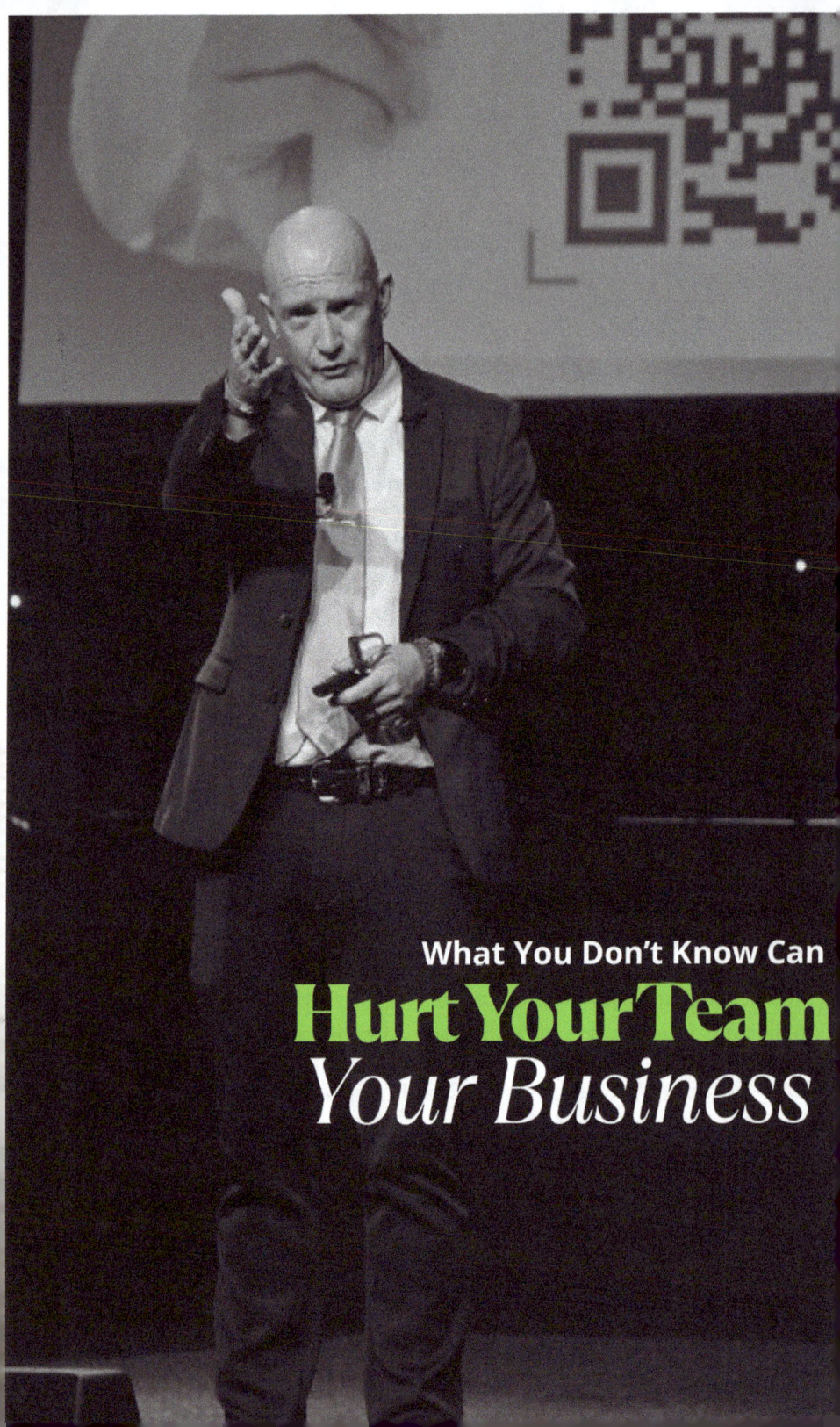

What You Don't Know Can
Hurt Your Team
Your Business

CHAPTER 3: THE COMPLIANCE AND LEGAL ASPECTS OF PSYCHOLOGICAL SAFETY

What You Don't Know Can Hurt Your Team – and Your Business

Let me say this as plainly as I can: Psychological safety is no longer just a leadership choice. It's a legal obligation.

In Australia, there's now a code of practice that explicitly links psychological safety to compliance. It's about risk. It's about duty of care. And yes, it's about you – the leader.

If your workplace is not psychologically safe, and that leads to harm? You could be held legally accountable. Let that sink in.
We're no longer in the 'nice to have' era. We're in the 'must do, or else' phase.

So this chapter isn't just about theory - it's about protection. For your people. For your culture. And yes, for your business.

Let's break it down using the 14 psychosocial hazards that every leader needs to know.

Note that there are two very valid reasons that I put this section under chapter 1 (in the Communication section).

One is because you need to know this information, and you need to be able to communicate it. You need to be able to have a discussion with your leader (yes, manage up), and talk through what areas of the legislation you are or are not complying with.

The second is that this information needs to be at the front of the book.

It needs to be here, because I presume that some readers are reading this just to work out how to comply, legally, with psychological safety regulations. Which is fine.

If that is you, this is your leave pass. Feel free to understand the 14 psychological hazards, then put this book down (or pass it onto another leader).

The 14 psychological hazards are your legal obligations. The remainder of the book is about your moral obligations. Your moral obligations as a leader to be a good human being.

The following 14 legal obligations are your ticket to both developing a more psychologically safe organisation (from a process perspective).

What Are Psychosocial Hazards?

They're aspects of work that could cause **psychological harm** – not just stress or discomfort, but long-term mental health impacts like anxiety, depression, burnout or trauma.

And if you ignore them, it's a compliance breach.

Each on the following 14 psychosocial hazards should be addressed with an organisational policy and procedure, which should outline the organisation's process for complying with each of the 14 obligations. Here's how each one plays out in real teams – and what you, as a leader, can do.

The 14 Psychosocial Hazards – and What to Do About Them

1. Job Demands

What it looks like: Unreasonable workloads, unrealistic deadlines, not enough resources.
Compliance Tip: Monitor workloads and redistribute tasks before burnout begins.
Real Life Example: 'Jas is doing the job of two people since we lost a team member. No one's replaced them – and she's cracking.'
Leadership move: Audit your team's workload. If one person's carrying the weight, rebalance. Ask: What do you need from me to make this sustainable?

2. Low Job Control

What it looks like: Micromanagement. No say in how or when work is done.

Compliance Tip: Involve your team in decisions that affect their work.

Real Life Example: I coached a team where every report had to be signed off by three managers. The analyst said, 'Why bother thinking for myself?'

Leadership move: Loosen the reins. Ask: *What parts of this project would you like to own?*

3. Poor Support

What it looks like: No guidance. No one to escalate to. Leadership is MIA.

Compliance Tip: Check in regularly and remove blockers early.

Real Life Example: A junior worker I coached said, 'My manager hasn't checked in with me once in three months.'

Leadership move: Book 1-on-1s – and don't cancel them. Even 15 minutes of undivided attention tells people: *You matter.*

4. Lack of Role Clarity

What it looks like: Confusion. Overlap. 'That's not my job' vs. 'I didn't know that *was* my job.'

Compliance Tip: Define and document roles, responsibilities, and reporting lines.

Real Life Example: In one workshop, three team members thought **they** were the lead on the same task. No wonder it stalled.

Leadership move: Revisit the RACI matrix (this is a tool that clearly shows who is Responsible, Accountable, Consulted, and Informed, for each task or decision).

Clear it up. Write it down.

5. Poor Organisational Change Management

What it looks like: Surprises. No communication. Resistance.

Compliance Tip: Communicate early, often, and with honesty – even if you don't have all the answers.

Real Life Example: A team told me, 'We found out about the restructure from a LinkedIn post.' Ouch.

Leadership move: Communicate early, even if the message is: *We don't know everything yet, but here's what we do know …*

6. Inadequate Reward and Recognition

What it looks like: Hard work going unnoticed. Promotions going to the wrong people.

Compliance Tip: Acknowledge contributions regularly – privately, and publicly.

Real Life Example: I asked a manager, 'When did you last say thank you to your team?' Long pause. 'Um … last Christmas?'"

Leadership move: Catch people doing things right. Say it. Write it. Celebrate it in public.

7. Poor Workplace Relationships

What it looks like: Cliques. Gossip. Passive-aggressive communication.

Compliance Tip: Set behavioural expectations and address issues early.

Real Life Example: A team had an inside joke that excluded one member daily. 'It's just banter,' they said. It wasn't.

Leadership move: Set team norms. Model respectful language. Call out behaviour that isolates or undermines.

8. Bullying

What it looks like: Intimidation, humiliation, persistent criticism.

Compliance Tip: Enforce zero tolerance and act swiftly on reports.

Real Life Example: I once heard a leader say, 'I like to keep my team on edge. It keeps them sharp.' No – it keeps them scared.

Leadership move: Educate your team on what bullying is – and isn't. Encourage reporting of bullying behaviour.

9. Harassment (including sexual harassment)

What it looks like: Unwelcome jokes. Inappropriate comments. Power plays.
Compliance Tip: Provide clear reporting channels and take reporting seriously.
Real Life Example: One female apprentice shared that a senior tradesman called her 'sweetheart' every day. 'It makes my skin crawl,' she said.
Leadership move: Don't brush off discomfort. Investigate. Escalate. Stop the behaviour.

10. Conflict or Poor Workplace Behaviour

What it looks like: Frequent arguments. Finger-pointing. Blame culture.
Compliance Tip: Address the issue, not the person – provide examples as part of the feedback and discipline process.
Real Life Example: In one team, issues were never addressed – they festered until someone exploded.
Leadership move: Use structured feedback models like SBI (Situation, Behaviour, Impact). Teach 'disagree and commit.'

11. Remote or Isolated Work

What it looks like: Disconnection. Loneliness. Lack of support.
Compliance Tip: Ensure that there is a process for regular check ins with team members who work remotely.
Real Life Example: A remote worker once told me, 'No one's called me in weeks. I could disappear and no one would know.'
Leadership move: Schedule connection time. Virtual coffees. Team chats. Send a check-in message that's not about work.

12. Violence and Aggression

What it looks like: Shouting. Threats. Physical intimidation.
Compliance Tip: Train your team to de-escalate and have clear

incident protocols.

Real Life Example: I've worked with frontline leaders who've faced this from customers and internal staff.

Leadership move: Have an escalation process. Train your team in dealing with aggressive behaviour. If it's happening, report it – and protect your people.

13. Traumatic Events or Material

What it looks like: Exposure to graphic, distressing, or emotionally heavy situations.

Compliance Tip: Offer EAP (Employee Assistance Programs), peer debriefs and support, and time to recover (whether it is work related or not).

Real Life Examples: This one often affects healthcare, emergency, and justice workers. But it also applies to redundancy, fatal incidents, or suicides.

Leadership move: Offer debriefing. Say, 'You don't have to process this alone.'

14. Poor Environmental Conditions

What it looks like: Noise, light, ventilation, temperature, or physical discomfort that causes stress or distraction.

Compliance Tip: Monitor environmental risks and act on reports promptly.

Real Life Example: As a young tradesman, I often worked in the steel housing of blast hole drills or face shovels on a mine site in remote Western Australia. It was 40 plus degrees Celsius outside, and we measured the temperature at 63 degree Celsius inside on one very hot day. That was unsafe (physically).

Leadership move: Fix the basics. Show that physical safety and comfort are priorities.

Bottom Line: If You Don't Name It, You Can't Change It

If you're thinking, 'We've got some of these,' that's normal. Most workplaces do.

The question is:

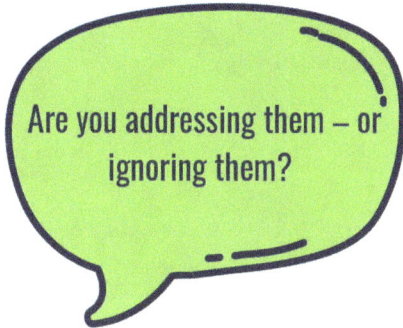

Are you addressing them – or ignoring them?

Psychological safety isn't about being perfect. It's about being proactive.

LEADER REFLECTION AND ACTIVITIES

- Step1: Download the Safe Work Australia psychosocial code of practice (or your local equivalent). Read it. Highlight what matters to your context.
- Step 2: Self-assess your team using the 14-hazard list above. Identify 1–2 areas you've seen signs of risk.
- Step 3: Book a conversation. Raise it. Say, 'I've noticed we might be at risk here, and I want us to be proactive.'
- Step 4: Document your actions. Not for cover – but for culture. To show your team: 'I take your safety seriously'.

COACH'S WRAP-UP

You're not expected to be a psychologist. But you are expected to be a protector. As a leader, your duty is to:

- Know the hazards
- Spot them in your team
- Talk about them
- Take action

If you're doing that? You're already ahead of the game. You're not just keeping your team safe – you're building a culture of trust, care and courage.

And if you're not? The consequences go beyond performance. They're legal. Reputational. Human.

So ask yourself:

What psychosocial hazard is quietly present in your team? What's one thing you can do this week to reduce that risk?

Then do it. Speak safe. Lead smart.

SECTION 2:

ACCEPTANCE

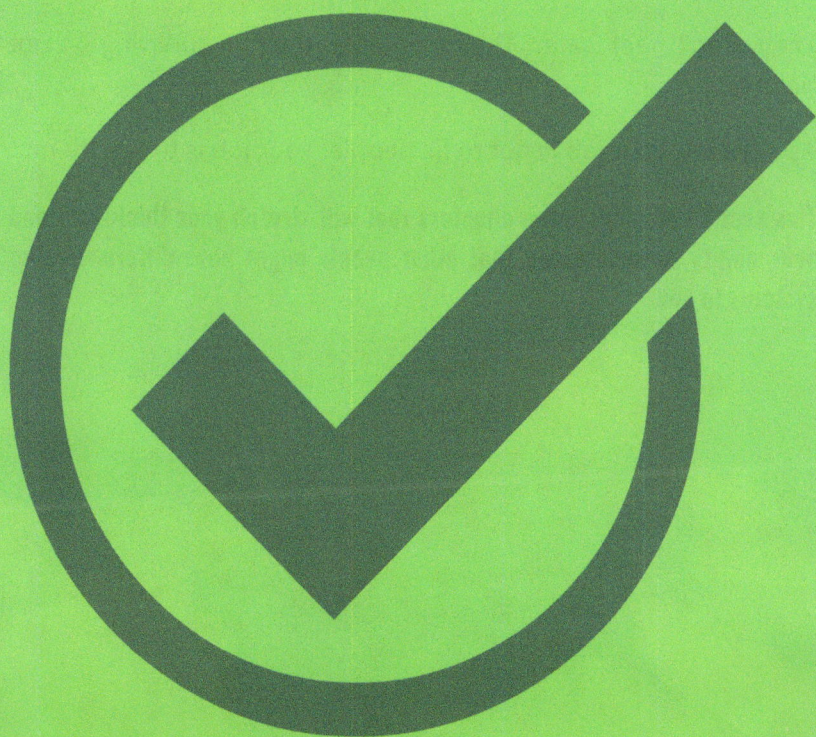

ACCEPTANCE

Acceptance is where safety becomes personal. It's where we move beyond words – and into **how we see, hear and honour each other.**

This section is about making space.

- Space for difference.
- Space for diversity.
- Space for disagreement.

Space for people to show up *as they really are* – not as a filtered, polished, corporate version of themselves.

Because when people feel they have to shrink, conform or camouflage just to 'fit in'?

They don't feel safe. They feel like they're surviving – not belonging.

As a leader, your job is not to fix people. Your job is to see them.

This section includes three chapters that will stretch your thinking – and your ability to understand that other people might have different belief systems to you.

LEADING HUMANS MEANS UNDERSTANDING HUMANS

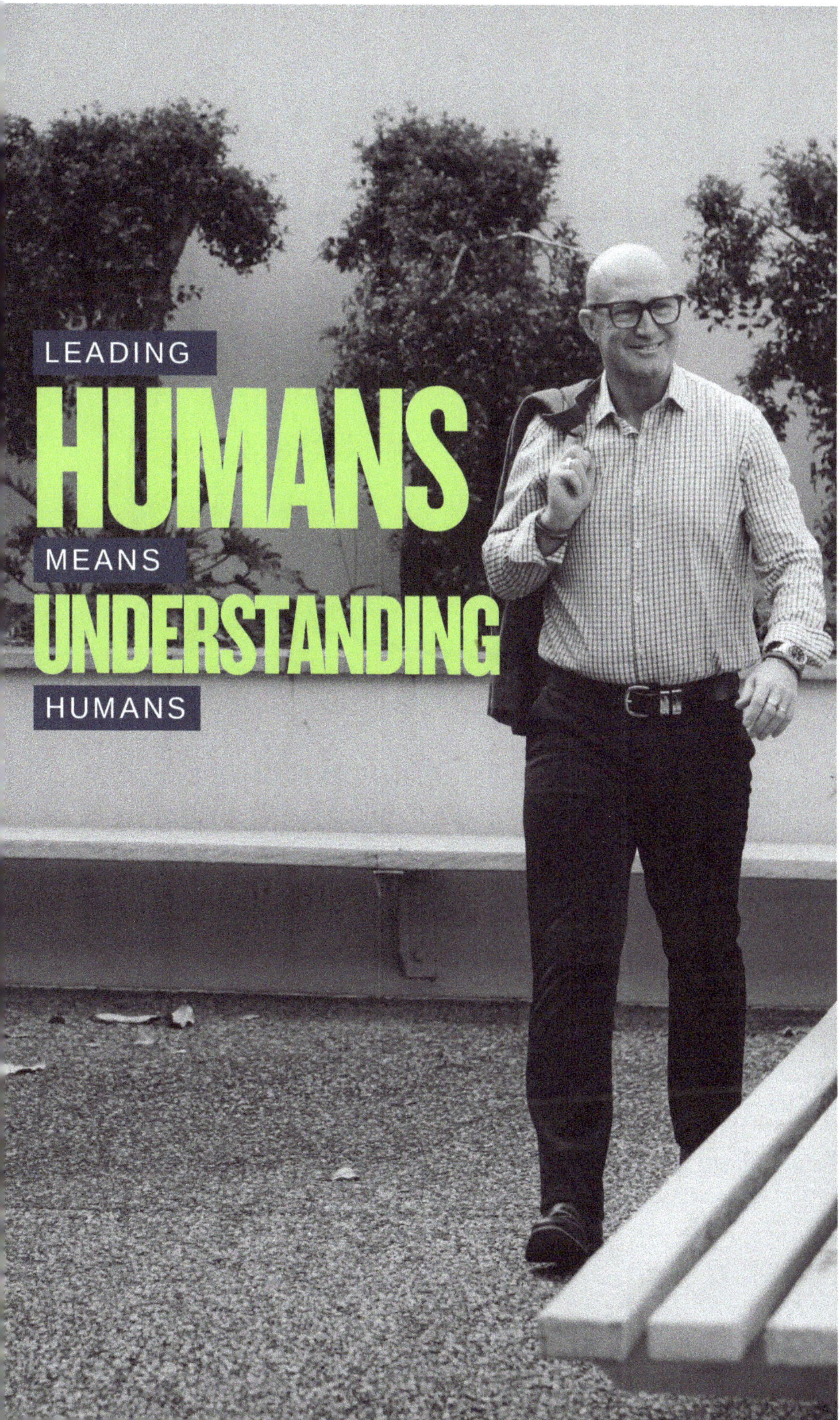

CHAPTER 4: EVERYONE IS DIFFERENT

Why Great Leaders Don't Lead Everyone the Same Way

Let me start with a truth I've said in almost every leadership workshop:

> 'You can't treat everyone the same and expect them to perform the same.'

Read that again.

Because if there's one thing that crushes psychological safety and team connection fast, it's *one-size-fits-all* leadership.

Every team member is different. Different personality. Different values. Different motivators. Different capacity. Different trauma. Different wiring.

And the leaders who ignore that? They lose people. Or worse – they lose people's trust while they're still on the payroll.

This chapter is your reminder that leading humans means understanding humans. It's about creating space for difference – and using it to build something better.

Surrounded by Idiots

In Surrounded by Idiots, author Thomas Erikson breaks down one of the simplest and most practical behavioural frameworks leaders can use to understand their teams: the DISC model.

The book's central message is clear:
People aren't difficult. They're just different.

And when you learn to recognise and respond to those differences, you stop getting frustrated – and start leading better.

Erikson describes four main communication and personality types, each represented by a colour:

- ● Red (Dominant) – Direct, fast-paced, focused on results
- ● Yellow (Influential) – Social, enthusiastic, driven by energy and ideas
- ● Green (Stable) – Supportive, loyal, values harmony and predictability
- ● Blue (Conscientious) – Analytical, detail-oriented, driven by precision

Here's the kicker:
Each type brings value.
Each type also brings tension – if you don't know how to work with them.

This framework doesn't put people in boxes. It helps you open the box of communication and motivation. It teaches you that your team isn't full of idiots. It's full of people who think, feel, and function differently than you – and that's exactly what makes them valuable.

Great leaders don't treat everyone the same.
They treat everyone *the way they need to be led.*
That's how you build trust, respect and psychological safety – through understanding, not assumption.

The 'Difficult' New Hire (A Coaching Scenario)

Let me introduce you to a fictional leader we'll call *Jason*. Jason's a site superintendent, ex-tradesman, straight shooter. Great track record. Solid values. And zero patience for what he calls 'fluff'.

Jason hires a new project officer, *Ella*. Super qualified. Neurodivergent. Prefers to process instructions in writing. Doesn't like big team meetings. Needs quiet space to think.

Two weeks in, Jason's frustrated.

'She's smart, but she's slow to respond. She zones out in meetings. I don't know if she's going to cut it.'

So I asked Jason one question:

'Do you want her to fit into your system, or do you want her to thrive?'

Silence.

Then I walked him through her DISC profile and explained how neurodiverse brains often process and communicate differently – not worse, just differently.

He shifted. He stopped holding big, chaotic meetings. He gave her agendas in advance. He checked in by email, not phone.
Four weeks later, Jason's words?

'She's a gun. She just needed a different way in.'

That's leadership maturity. That's psychological safety.

The Psychology of Individual Differences

In her research, **Amy Edmondson** reminds us that safety isn't the same for everyone. What feels safe for one team member (speaking in front of a crowd) might feel terrifying to another.

And as **Timothy R. Clark** puts it in *The 4 Stages of Psychological Safety* – you don't get contributor safety until you've created inclusion safety. And inclusion safety means people feel accepted as they are.

That means:
- Introverts don't have to 'speak up more'.
- Neurodiverse thinkers don't have to 'work like everyone else'.
- Emerging leaders don't need to 'fake confidence' to be seen.

They just need space to bring their best selves forward. And that's your job.

Personal Insight: When Everything Changed

I haven't always thought the way I do now.
In fact, the way I lead, coach, and speak about safety was shaped in a moment I'll never forget – the day I survived an electrical explosion.

I was young. I was confident. I believed I knew enough to keep myself safe.

But on that day, one wrong assumption, one unconscious belief, and one missed protocol nearly cost me my life. I was burned. Badly.

It changed everything – physically, mentally, professionally. That experience didn't just hurt.

It shattered my belief system around safety, leadership and responsibility.

I realised I'd been relying on a mindset of:
- 'She'll be right'
- 'I've done this before'
- 'I know what I'm doing'

Those weren't just thoughts. They were beliefs – and they were driving my behaviour.

And that's what this next section is about.

Every single person has a different belief system, and acceptance helps leaders to understand that.

Personal Insight: When Everything Changed

I have since studied a Psychology Degree, and I understand that our beliefs drive our behaviours, which drive our consequences. In other words, how we think, shows up in how we act, shows up in the outcomes we get.

We all operate from **internal belief systems** – we all have deeply held ideas about:

- What's safe and what's risky
- What's worth speaking up about and what's 'not my place'
- Who gets to lead and who should stay quiet
- What it means to make a mistake
- Whether it's better to be honest … or to be liked

These beliefs come from our upbringing, our culture, our trauma, our habits and the stories we tell ourselves.

If we don't examine them, they run us.

If we do, we can choose better ones.

So as you move through this next section, I invite you to reflect on your own belief systems – especially the ones you've never questioned.

Because psychological safety isn't just about what you *do*. It's about what you *believe* – and what you help others believe about themselves.

Where it all started for me

In 2004, I was asked to share the story of my electrical incident at a safety meeting. I loved the experience that much, I quit my job, and started a business as a 'Safety Speaker'.

I chose to become a safety speaker that day because I realised my story could save someone else's life. After surviving a serious incident at the age of 21, I walked away physically scarred but mentally transformed.

That incident forced me to take a hard look at the decisions I'd made, the culture I'd worked in, and the beliefs that nearly cost me everything. At first, I shared my experience with small crews and toolbox talks – just hoping to help someone think twice. But as I spoke, people leaned in.

They didn't just hear the story – they felt it. That's when I knew: this wasn't just about safety procedures. It was about human psychology, leadership and the conversations we weren't having. That's where my speaking journey began – and why I've never stopped.

The problem that I faced was that some people didn't lean in. They struggled with the mindset change that I was talking about. They had a different belief system. Which I could understand.

That was my first experience with acceptance and knowing that mindset change and belief change is a very different journey for every person.

Negative beliefs

After about five years of hearing both very positive responses to my safety story, and very (very) negative responses – not everyone is excited to hear a safety speaker, I documented all of the negative beliefs that I heard.

I knew that leaders would be hearing these as well, so I wrote a book on how to have safety conversations (in the field) with people that don't believe in the safety process.

Every chapter of the book was about a negative belief, and how as a leader, you could respond to those beliefs. The book is the conversation manual for leaders who want to have safety conversations in an accepting way

While at the same time keeping people safe.

Here are the chapter headings, and the types of beliefs that I heard in the first five years of my safety speaking work.

To this day, I still get asked to tell my story.

And I still sell copies of the book *'Let's Talk About Safety (19 ways you can work more safely)'*.

Here are the chapter headings, to highlight some of the beliefs that people have – and you'll have to read the book, to understand how you would respond to those beliefs in more detail.

Think about how you might respond to people if they made the following comments, or had the following belief systems. How would you respond, with acceptance, and with responsibility and empathy.

1. Anton, I just don't have time to work safely; we have to get the job done.
2. Anton, I never follow procedures because they're all wrong or not worth using.
3. Anton, they always put production before safety here ... they say one thing, but do another.
4. Anton, it won't happen to me. Look, I know how to do my job. I've been doing it this way for years.

5. Anton, safety is not my responsibility. It is the company's responsibility.
6. Anton, I sometimes forget the importance of the choices I make at work.
7. Anton, I work safely, but my team members take risks.
8. Anton, if I get hurt, it won't matter; it'll only be me that suffers.
9. Anton, no matter what you do, you can't prevent accidents or incidents. Something will always happen.
10. Anton, it's just too much of a hassle to report a near-miss; you end up being treated like a criminal.
11. Anton, if I try to talk to my workmates about safety, they might tell me to 'bugger off'.
12. Anton, I only do 'safety stuff' because I have to, not because I want to or see value in it.
13. Anton, I heard you had an incident at work. What happened?
14. Anton, my managers aren't serious about safety. They don't put enough time, energy, or resources into it.
15. Anton, the only reason we have safety systems around here is because the managers want to cover their arse.
16. Anton, if I work safely, my team members think I'm stupid and ridicule me.
17. Anton, it's great when I have to do some work at home; I don't have to do all the safety stuff, I can just hop in and get it done!
18. Anton, where to from here? How can I apply some of the things we've been discussing?
19. Anton, thanks for the chat. How else can I apply the information we've discussed?

Not everyone I spoke to had these belief systems. Some did.

In that book, I dedicate one paragraph to each of the above conversations. Most of the conversations focus on consequences, and how those belief systems could lead to the person getting badly injured.

Hearing so many different belief systems highlighted early in my speaking career that everyone is very different.

I needed to change my communication style for every single person I spoke to.

What 'Everyone Is Different' Looks Like in Real Teams

Let's break down what this actually means day-to-day.

Communication Styles

- **Some team members need time to think before responding.** Others will talk to process out loud.
- **Some prefer to write.** Others need face-to-face to feel heard.
- **Some will challenge you directly.** Others will shut down unless invited.

Your job? Tune in. Ask how they prefer to communicate. Then adapt.

Workload Preferences

- **Some love big projects with lots of ambiguity.** Others thrive on clear roles, defined tasks, and structure.
- **Some recharge with people.** Others recharge with solo time.

Your job? Match the task to the temperament, where you can.

Emotional Range

- **Some wear their stress on their sleeve.** Others hide it behind smiles – or silence.
- **Some crave recognition.** Others feel embarrassed by public praise.

Your job? Pay attention to reactions. Ask instead of assuming.

The Myth of 'Fair Means Same'

Leaders often say,

'I treat everyone the same.'

And while that might sound noble, here's what it really does: it flattens the difference.

Here's the truth:

Fair doesn't mean *same*. Fair means *equitable*.

Equity is giving each person what they need to succeed – even if it looks different from what you give someone else.

Imagine a toolbox. If one person needs a hammer and the other needs a screwdriver, giving them both hammers isn't 'fair'. It's lazy.

Your role is to know your people – and hand them the right tool.

COACHING ACTIVITY:

PROFILE THE HECK OUT OF YOUR TEAM

I say this all the time: 'Profile the heck out of your team'. It's one of the most practical things you can do.
Whether it's:

- **DISC**
- **Team Management Systems (TMS)**
- **Lifestyles Inventory (LSI)**
- Or just your own structured check-ins

The more you understand how your team ticks, the better you lead.

Ask questions like:
- What kind of feedback works best for you?
- How do you prefer to communicate?
- What energises you at work?
- What drains you?

Then *document* what you learn. Review it before 1-on-1s. Use it when allocating work. Bring it up when tensions rise.

People feel safe when they feel seen.

If you would like profile your team, reach out to our office, and we will get you and your team set up with your DISC, TMS or LSI profile.

Celebrating Difference versus Tolerating It

One of the biggest shifts you can make as a leader is moving from tolerance to *curiosity.*

It's one thing to 'put up with' your team's quirks. It's another thing to 'understand' them.

It's the ultimate leadership skill to leverage them.
Want to build psychological safety?

Start praising:
- The analyst who double-checks everything.
- The technician who questions the brief.
- The apprentice who quietly gets the job done while others grandstand.

Let people know:

'You're not just accepted here – you're valued for who you are.'

Leading Across Generations: All Four of Them (at times)

Another layer of difference that matters in leadership? Generational identity.

For the first time in history, many workplaces have four or five generations working side-by-side – from Baby Boomers and Gen Xers, to Millennials, and now Gen Z.

And with that comes different expectations, communication styles, and views on things like:
- Work-life balance
- Feedback frequency
- Technology use
- Respect and authority
- Career progression

If you've ever thought, 'Why don't they just do it the way we used to?' or 'Why is this taking so long to explain?' – you're not alone.

But here's what leadership expert Lindsay Pollak reminds us in her book The Remix:

'Generational differences are real, but they're not obstacles – they're opportunities to learn, grow, and connect more deeply.'

She encourages leaders to 'be the bridge' – to flex across styles, to listen more than you assume, and to adjust your leadership like you'd adjust your tone for someone learning a second language.

Because what works for a Baby Boomer might frustrate a Gen Z team member. And what energises a Millennial might confuse your Gen X colleague.

It's not about bending over backwards.
It's about leading with curiosity, not criticism.

LEADER REFLECTION AND ACTIVITIES

Prompt 1: Map Your Team
- List every direct report.
- Write down 1–2 things you know about their working style.
- Identify any blanks – what don't you know?

Prompt 2: Your Default Bias
- Do you favour team members who think like you?
- Do you unconsciously dismiss those who don't?
- What's one behaviour you can change to make more room?

Practice Challenge:
- Ask one team member this week:
- *'What's something I could do differently to support you better?'*

Then listen. Thank them. And try it.

COACH'S WRAP-UP

People aren't problems to fix – they're puzzles to understand. And great leaders don't flatten the curve of human difference – they *lean into it*.

When you acknowledge differences ... When you communicate based on preference ... When you stop managing to the middle and start leading at the edges ...

That's when safety builds. That's when trust deepens. That's when performance skyrockets. So the next time you catch yourself thinking, *'Why can't they just ...'* – stop.

Replace it with: *'What might they need to thrive?'* Then lead them that way.

Because everyone is different. And that's your leadership superpower – if you choose to use it.

CHAPTER 5: ALL VOICES SHOULD BE HEARD

Making It Safe for Everyone to Speak – Not Just the Loudest

If you want to know how psychologically safe a team is, don't look at how much the leader talks.

Look at how much the *quietest team member* contributes.

Look at who's speaking in meetings – and who never does.
Look at whether ideas are volunteered – or extracted.
Look at whether feedback is shared – or feared.

One of the most powerful leadership lessons I've learned is this:

The smartest, most game-changing ideas in your team are often sitting in the head of the person who speaks the least.

And if you don't create space for that voice – you lose the idea. You lose the insight.

Eventually, you might lose the person too.

This chapter is about fixing that. Because real leadership isn't just about having a voice – it's about making space for others to use theirs.

The Analyst Who Saved the Day (True Story, Fictionalised)

I once worked with a high-performing project team – tight deadlines, major budgets and big personalities.

During a critical pre-start, the project manager was outlining the next phase of a structural install.

Everyone nodded.

Except for one junior analyst – *Arjun*. Brilliant. Detail-focused. Quiet.

He hesitated. Raised a hand slightly. The PM didn't see it. Kept talking.

Arjun didn't speak.

At the end of the meeting, a senior engineer happened to ask, 'Anything else?'

Arjun, nervously:
'I noticed in the drawings ... the load distribution isn't consistent. I think the frame might flex.'

Silence.

They checked. He was right. A full redesign was needed.

That comment – mumbled, late, almost lost – saved the business *millions*.

But what stuck with me wasn't the insight. It was this:
'I almost didn't say anything. I didn't think it was my place.'

That's a leadership failure.
No one had said Arjun's voice didn't matter.
But no one had *shown* him it did either.

The Psychology of Voice

Let's tap into the research for a second.

In Amy Edmondson's studies on psychological safety, one thing becomes clear again and again:

People don't speak up when they fear rejection, humiliation, or repercussion.

And fear doesn't need to be loud. It can be quiet.
- A look.
- A sigh.
- A rushed meeting.
- A dominant peer who always talks first.

Fear silences.

Timothy R. Clark also reminds us that contributor safety – the stage where people actively offer ideas – isn't automatic. It has to be invited. Repeatedly. Safely. Consistently.

As a leader, that's your work.

Why People Don't Speak Up

It's not always about fear of punishment. Sometimes it's more subtle. Here are five common reasons team members stay silent:

1. **'I don't think it's my place.'**
   Especially true for junior staff, introverts, or contractors.
2. **'They've already made up their mind.'**
   If meetings feel like a performance, not a conversation, people opt out.
3. **'Last time I spoke up, it backfired.'**
   A dismissive comment, a snarky reply, or a leader's eye-roll – these moments linger.

4. **'Someone else will probably say it.'**
   Groupthink takes over. Everyone assumes someone else will raise the concern.
5. **'I don't know how to say it properly.'**
   Fear of stumbling, not being articulate, or being misunderstood.

Your job as a leader is to *remove these barriers.*

Leadership Habits That Unlock Voice

Let's get tactical. Here are practical behaviours that make it safe – and expected – for all voices to be heard.

1. Create Speaking Rotations
In team meetings, invite different people to lead agenda items or summarise discussions. Don't let the same three voices dominate.

'Arjun, what are you seeing from the data side of things?'

2. Ask for Input Before the Meeting
Not everyone processes ideas in real time. Give introverts and deep thinkers time to reflect.

'We're discussing the Q3 forecast on Thursday. Feel free to send your thoughts before the meeting.'

3. Make Silence Safe
Say this early and often:

'Just because you're quiet doesn't mean your input isn't valued. We'll always make time for your views.'

Then prove it.

4. Normalise Unpolished Ideas
Let your team know: it doesn't have to be perfect to be valuable.

'We're not looking for polished pitches here – just thoughts, sparks or concerns.'

5. Back Up the Brave
When someone speaks up – especially if it's a challenge or risk flag – publicly support them.

'Thanks for calling that out. That's exactly what we need more of.'

Dealing with the Dominators

Every team has one: the person who jumps in first, talks the longest, or interrupts constantly.

They're not always malicious – they're just unaware. But they create silence around them.

You don't need to shut them down. You just need to redirect them.

Try:
- 'Let's hear from a few others before we circle back to you.'
- 'I want to give space for people who haven't spoken yet.'

If needed, have the 1-on-1:
'You bring great energy and insight – I'd love your help in making sure others have space too.'

Coaching Snapshot: Elevating the Quiet Achiever

I coached a leader, Janelle, whose team included Cam, a brilliant but quiet technician. Never volunteered ideas. Avoided conflict. Seemed disengaged.

In a 1-on-1, Janelle asked him:
'You've been in these meetings for six months – what's something you've noticed that we haven't?'

Cam replied:
'Honestly? We solve the wrong problem first. Then we spend weeks fixing the thing we ignored.'

Boom.

They ran with Cam's insight. Processes changed. Results improved.

Janelle gave him public credit. Later, Cam led a working group.

He didn't need to 'speak more'. He needed someone to ask and listen.

LEADER REFLECTION AND ACTIVITIES

Ask yourself:

- Who in my team do I hear from the most?
- Who do I rarely hear from?
- Is that balance reflective of contribution – or comfort?
- What have I done to invite different voices in the past 30 days?

Then do something about it.

Activity 1: The 'Who Haven't I Heard From?' List

- Write down your team.
- Circle the names you hear from often.
- Put a star next to those you haven't heard from recently.

Now plan a conversation with one of the starred names this week. Ask:

'What's something we should be talking about that we aren't?'

Activity 2: The 60-Second Roundtable
- In your next meeting, pick a topic and give everyone 60 seconds to share their view – no interruptions, no crosstalk.
- Debrief: What surprised you? What did you learn?

Activity 3: The Praise Ping
- This week, publicly recognise someone *for their voice.*
- Say: 'I really appreciated what [Name] shared earlier – let's all take a note from that.'

COACH'S WRAP-UP

It's easy to listen to the loudest. It takes *leadership* to hear the quietest.

Inclusion isn't just about who's in the room.
It's about who *gets airtime.*

So your challenge is this:

Don't just invite voices. Make space for them. Don't just tolerate ideas. Celebrate them. Don't just hear – *listen.*

Because when all voices are heard, teams get smarter.
Faster. Safer.

Better. And your job? Is to go first.

CHAPTER 6: BOUNDARIES ARE IMPORTANT

Why Saying 'No' (or 'Not Now') Creates Safer, Stronger Teams

Let me ask you something that might hit a nerve:

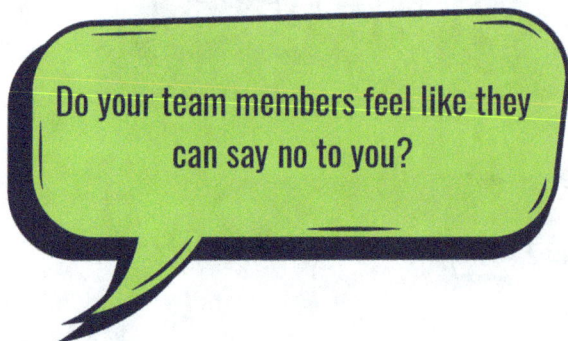

> Do your team members feel like they can say no to you?

If that question made your gut clench, that's the sign right there.

Because psychological safety isn't just about speaking up with ideas – it's also about setting limits. Saying, 'I'm overloaded.' Saying, 'I need help.' Saying, 'That's outside my role right now.'

And if your people don't feel like they can set those boundaries with you?
You don't have safety.
You have compliance.

And here's the kicker:
Boundaries aren't barriers.
They're *frameworks* for respect.
They tell your team: 'You're allowed to protect your time, your wellbeing, and your values.'

This chapter is about helping you – and your team – get better at that.

The Manager Who Was Always Available (Until He Wasn't)

Let's start with a fictionalised-but-familiar example from a coaching call I had with a leader named Craig.

Craig was an operations lead. Passionate. Driven. Big heart. Always said yes. 'Open door policy,' he told me. 'My team knows I'm here, 24/7.'

Sounds great, right?

Except …
His phone buzzed non-stop.
He had meetings from 7AM to 7PM.
He was burning out.

And worse – his team had stopped solving problems on their own. Why bother? Craig was always there to 'handle it.'

So we dug in.

'Craig, when did you last say no to a task, a request, or a meeting?'

He paused. 'I … honestly don't remember.'

And that was the problem. Not just for Craig, but for his team.

He wasn't leading – he was rescuing. He was solving, not empowering.

And underneath it all?
He was afraid that setting boundaries would make him look less available.

When in fact, it would've made him more *effective.*

What Boundaries Actually Do (Psychologically)

Boundaries tell people:
- 'You matter.'
- 'Your needs are valid.'
- 'This space, time, or energy is worth protecting.'

Boundaries also signal *predictability* – a cornerstone of psychological safety.

Think about it:
- When a leader says yes to everything, the team learns nothing is sacred – not deadlines, not priorities, not people's time.
- When meetings run over every day, the message is: *Your time is mine to use.*
- When messages ping at 9:47PM and the response is immediate, the message is: *We don't rest here.*

You might think you're being supportive. But what you're actually building is tension, chaos, and co-dependency.

Amy Edmondson calls this the 'mutual learning environment.' For that to exist, people need to know when it's safe to engage – and when it's okay to pause.

Boundaries create that rhythm.

What Boundary-Less Leadership Looks Like

Here are some red flags I see all the time in teams that lack boundary culture:

1. **'Everything is urgent.'** There's no prioritisation. No triage. Everything is a fire.
2. **'Everyone is available, all the time.'** Weekends, public holidays, birthdays – nothing is off-limits.
3. **'Meetings never end on time.'** Time disrespect becomes the norm.
4. **'People say yes – but resent it.'** There's unspoken resistance, even as tasks pile up.

5. **'Breaks feel like betrayal.'** If someone leaves on time or declines a meeting, they're seen as lazy.

That's not a high-performance culture.
That's a high-pressure one.

And here's the thing: pressure eventually breaks.

How Great Leaders Set – and Model – Boundaries

Boundaries are not rules you impose on others.
They're agreements you model, reinforce and respect.

Here's how to lead the way:

1. Be Explicit About Your Own Boundaries
Say it out loud:
'I don't check emails after 6PM. If it's urgent, call me directly.'
You're not being rigid. You're being clear. And clear is kind.

2. Ask for Others' Boundaries
Try this in your next 1-on-1:

'Are there any work habits or communication times that feel off for you?'

You'd be amazed what you'll learn:
- 'I struggle with back-to-back meetings.'
- 'I need uninterrupted time to write reports.'
- 'I do school pick-up from 3–4PM.'

Respecting that doesn't lower performance.
It *unlocks* it.

3. Protect Time
Block calendar time for your own focused work – and protect it like you would a meeting with the CEO.

Even better? Teach your team to do the same.
'I've set aside 10–12 as deep work time. I encourage you to claim space like that too.'

4. Role Model 'No'

Saying no (or 'not now') is powerful leadership.

You could say:
- 'I can't take this on right now – what can we shift to make it work?'
- 'Let's park this until next week. We've got too much on today.'
- 'I'd rather do one thing well than rush five things badly.'

Boundaries aren't excuses.
They're *filters for focus.*

Coaching Snapshot: Resetting Team Expectations

I once worked with a marketing leader, Sarah, whose team was running hot. Always on. Slack messages at all hours. Frayed nerves. High turnover.

She told her team:
'We've been operating in a way that's unsustainable. That's on me. I want to reset.'

She introduced:
- Core hours: 9AM–4PM
- No-meeting Fridays
- Daily 'no interruption' time from 2–3PM
- Email cut-off at 6PM

Some resisted at first. But within two weeks?
- Morale lifted.
- Work quality improved.
- People smiled again.

Boundaries didn't limit them.
They *liberated* them.

Coaching Snapshot: Resetting Team Expectations

Not sure how to say it? Try these:

WITH A TEAM MEMBER WHO'S OVERLOADED:

'It looks like your plate's full. Let's figure out what needs to shift.'

WHEN SOMEONE KEEPS WORKING LATE:

'I notice you're staying back a lot – how can we make that more sustainable?'

IF SOMEONE PUSHES YOUR BOUNDARIES:

'I want to support you, but I also need to stay within my limits. Can we plan this for tomorrow?'

WHEN SETTING TEAM-WIDE NORMS:

'Let's talk about what healthy working boundaries look like for us as a team.'

LEADER REFLECTION AND ACTIVITIES

Activity 1: Map Your Current Boundaries

What are your boundaries around:

- Time?
- Availability?
- Communication?
- Emotional energy?

Write them down.

Now ask: 'Have I communicated these clearly? Or just hoped people respect them?'

Activity 2: Boundary Check-In With Your Team

Ask in your next team meeting:

- 'What working habits feel helpful?'
- 'Where do we overextend?'
- 'What's one thing we could do to protect time, energy or focus better?'

Document the ideas. Turn them into a shared agreement.

Activity 3: Role Modelling Challenge

This week, choose one boundary to model clearly. For example:

- Don't respond to messages after hours.
- Start a meeting by ending it on time.
- Say no to a low-priority request – and explain why.

Then reflect:

- How did it feel?
- What did your team notice?
- What impact did it have?

COACH'S WRAP-UP

You don't build safety by being endlessly available.
You build it by being consistently human.

Boundaries tell people:

- I respect my time – and yours.
- I want us to work hard, and rest hard too.
- I want high performance, not constant pressure.

Remember:
Burnout is not a badge of honour.
Chaos is not a culture.
And availability is not the same as leadership.

Set the tone. Set the rhythm. Set the boundaries.

Your team – and your nervous system – will thank you.

SECTION 3:

RESPONSIBILITY

RESPONSIBILITY

Psychological safety doesn't just happen because people feel accepted. It happens because leaders take responsibility for creating a culture where people know:

- Where they stand.
- What's expected.
- What will be tolerated – and what won't.

That their trust won't be broken the moment pressure hits. This section is about how you show up – not just when things are easy, but when things are messy.

It is about taking radical responsibility for your communication, and its impact on others.

Taking responsibility as a leader aligns closely with the concept of **Extreme Ownership**, as taught by **Jocko Willink and Leif Babin** in their bestselling book of the same name.

In *Extreme Ownership*, the authors – both former Navy SEAL commanders – argue that true leaders own everything in their world, especially the outcomes.

Similarly, in psychologically safe teams, leaders take responsibility not just for performance, but for culture, clarity, and communication. It's not about blame – it's about owning the space, the tone, and the impact you have on your people, every day.

Because if safety is about creating connection, then responsibility is about upholding it. It's the work of:

- Leading with your values
- Earning trust (and re-earning it when you get it wrong)
- Modelling integrity in every meeting, decision, and follow-through

This is where leadership grows up.

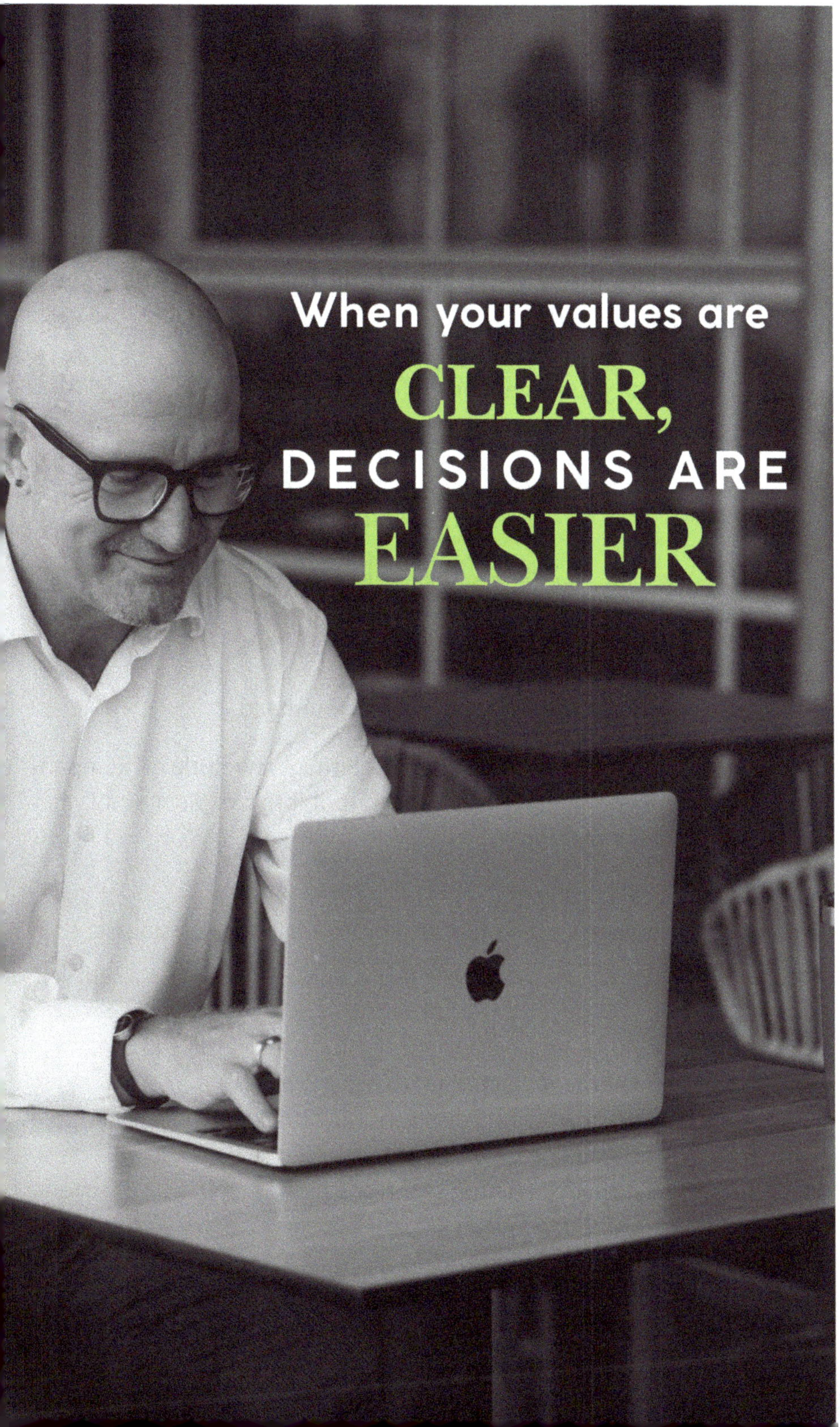
When your values are
CLEAR,
DECISIONS ARE
EASIER

CHAPTER 7: LEADING FROM YOUR VALUES

When You Know What You Stand For, People Know They Can Stand With You

Let me ask you something up front – and be honest:

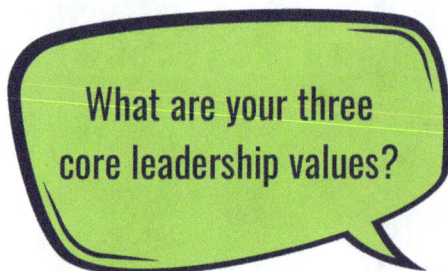

What are your three core leadership values?

Go on – name them. Out loud or in your head.

Most leaders I ask pause. Some squirm. A few rattle off company values like 'integrity' or 'respect,' but can't explain what they *personally* stand for.

And that's a problem.
Because values aren't just corporate wallpaper or slogans on a wall.

They're your leadership GPS.

They guide how you act when things get hard.
They influence every decision you make – especially the uncomfortable ones.
And they shape whether your team sees you as consistent, confusing, or hypocritical.

This chapter is about reconnecting with what actually drives you – so that your leadership is built on rock, not sand.

Why Values Matter in Leadership

Here's what I tell leaders in almost every session:

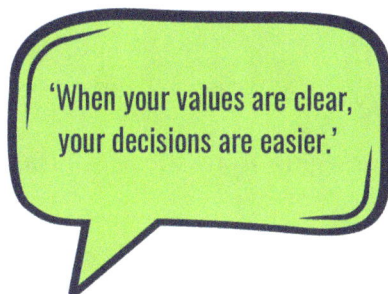

> 'When your values are clear, your decisions are easier.'

Think about the last time you were in a tough spot as a leader.
Maybe you had to call out poor behaviour.
Maybe you had to push back on your boss. Maybe you had to walk away from a role.

What got you through?

It probably wasn't a policy or a spreadsheet. It was *something in you* – a gut feeling that said, 'This is right,' or 'This is not okay.'

That gut feeling?
That's your values doing their job.

Coaching Case: When Values Are Violated

Let me tell you about **Anna** – a regional manager I worked with who had to let a long-serving staff member go due to repeated misconduct.

She'd put off the decision for weeks. 'He's been with us for 17 years,' she said. 'He knows everyone. He's ... part of the place.'
But he was also undermining colleagues, gossiping and pushing ethical boundaries.

Eventually, I asked her:
'What would you want your team to say about you after this?'

She said:
'That I did what was right. That I was fair. That I protected the team.'

Boom. There it was. *Her values.*
Fairness. Courage. Accountability.

We crafted her messaging from those values. She delivered it with clarity and calm.

And afterward? Her team said:
'We knew that must have been hard. But you did the right thing.'

That's values-based leadership in action.

Values and Psychological Safety

So how do values tie into psychological safety?

Amy Edmondson teaches that safety comes from *consistency and credibility*. When leaders behave in line with their stated beliefs, teams feel secure – even when the decisions are tough.

Timothy R. Clark also notes that trust is strongest when leaders live their values out loud.

HERE'S THE FORMULA:

Values	Alignment	Trust	Safety

But here's the catch: you can't live your values if you don't know what they are.

Discovering (or Reclaiming) Your Values

If you've never done a proper values exercise, now's the time.
Try this:

1. **Google 'list of personal values'.** (Or use the list I can send you.)
2. **Circle 10 words** that resonate deeply.
3. **Narrow it down to 3.** Ask: Which ones drive how I lead, not just how I want to feel?

For example:

- If you circled **integrity**, ask: Do I tell the truth, even when it costs me?
- If you circled **growth**, ask: Do I create opportunities for others to develop?
- If you circled **courage**, ask: Do I speak up when it would be easier to stay quiet?

Then write them down. Put them somewhere visible.
Because values only matter when they're visible, lived and felt.

What Living Your Values Looks Like

Let's get practical. Here's how values-based leadership plays out.

Value: Integrity
- You follow through.
- You admit when you're wrong.
- You hold others accountable – even your favourites.

Value: Service
- You lead from behind.
- You ask, 'How can I help?' more than 'What are you doing?'

Value: Curiosity
- You listen more than you talk.
- You create space for different views.
- You ask questions instead of assuming.

- You don't gossip.
- You give feedback with care.
- You honour people's time, boundaries and dignity.

Don't just say your values.
Let your team see them in action.

The Cost of Values Misalignment

Ever worked for a leader who preached one thing but practiced another?

Said they value 'openness' but shut down every hard conversation?

Claimed 'teamwork' but made every win about themselves?
It's jarring. Confusing. Demoralising.

And if that gap goes unaddressed? Trust disappears. Safety plummets. Performance suffers.

Your team is always watching. They notice the gap between what you say and what you do.

Close the gap, by addressing it.

Close the gap, by upskilling your leadership.

Upskilling Your Leadership Starts With You

One of the biggest truths I've come to believe – and write about in Upskill Your Leadership – is this:

'You can't lead others well if you're not leading yourself first.'

Before you can create psychological safety in your team, you need to build personal clarity, self-awareness and emotional control. That's the inner work of leadership. It's not always visible – but it's always felt.

- If you don't know your own values, how will you make decisions when the pressure's on?
- If you're not managing your energy, how will you hold space for your team's emotions?
- If you haven't developed resilience, how will you model it when the unexpected hits?

Upskilling your leadership isn't about taking another course or learning another model. It's about upgrading your *inner game* – so your outer leadership reflects consistency, confidence and care.

In *Upskill Your Leadership,* I guide leaders to uncover their leadership style, define their non-negotiables, and develop the habits that make them better humans *and* better leaders.

When you do that work, something powerful happens:
You don't just lead your team.
You lead with integrity.
You lead with presence.
You lead in a way that *creates safety without needing to say it out loud.*

Coaching Prompt: Your Values in the Wild

Ask yourself:
- What's one recent decision that aligned beautifully with your values?
- What's one decision that felt off – and why?
- Where are you compromising a value right now?

You don't need to fix it all today. Just notice. Name it. Then decide what to do with that information.

From Values to Culture

Here's a powerful leadership move: share your values with your team.

Literally say:
'These are the three values that guide my leadership. I'd love for us to build this culture together.'

Then ask:
'What values matter most to you?'

Turn it into a team conversation. A living agreement. A shared compass.

When values are named, aligned, and reinforced – they become culture.

And culture becomes safety.

Radical Candour: Say the Hard Thing – With Heart

One of the biggest responsibilities that leaders have, is the responsibility to use radical candour during conversations.
Particularly when delivering feedback.
For team members, one of the most powerful things leaders can do is give honest, helpful feedback. But most leaders weren't taught how to do it well.
We're either too soft – tiptoeing around the truth because we're scared of hurting someone's feelings.

Or we're too blunt – saying the right thing in the wrong way and leaving people shut down instead of lifted up.

Radical Candour, a concept created by leadership expert and former Google/Apple exec Kim Scott, offers a third path. A better path.

It's about learning how to:
'Care personally and challenge directly.'

Not one or the other.
Both.

What Radical Candour Is – And What It's Not

Scott lays out four feedback quadrants based on two axes:
- Caring personally
- Challenging directly

Only when both are present do we operate in the Radical Candour zone.

Here's how the four quadrants break down:

Quadrant	What It Feels Like
Radical Candour	'I care about you, so I'm going to be honest.'
Ruinous Empathy	'I care, so I'll avoid hurting you … even if it hurts the team.'
Obnoxious Aggression	'Here's the truth—but I don't really care how it lands.'
Manipulative Insincerity	'I'll say whatever's easiest or most self-serving.'

Scott warns that most leaders accidentally live in Ruinous Empathy – where we avoid tough conversations to spare someone's feelings. But avoiding the hard thing isn't kind. It's just *comfortable.*

'Radical Candour is measured not at your mouth, but at the other person's ear.' – *Kim Scott*

It's not about how *right* you are. It's about whether your message lands with clarity and care.

LEADER REFLECTION AND ACTIVITIES

Activity 1: Identify Your Values

- Step 1: Google 'list of core personal values' or use a worksheet.
- Step 2: Circle 10. Then narrow it down to 3.
- Step 3: Write each one down and finish this sentence:

'To me, this value means ...'

'I live this value by ...'

'When I violate this value, I feel ...'

'A leader I admire who lives this value is ...'

Activity 2: The Alignment Audit

Think about:

- One decision you're currently wrestling with.
- One area where you're feeling internal tension.
- One relationship that feels 'off.'

Now ask:

'Is there a values conflict here?'

Write down what you discover. Then consider what action might bring you back into alignment.

Activity 3: Give Feedback

Think about:

- Caring personally
- Challenging directly
- Being clear, while communicating with care

Now ask:

'Is there a values conflict here?'

Write down what you discover. Then consider what action might bring you back into alignment.

COACH'S WRAP-UP

If you remember nothing else from this chapter, remember this:

> You lead best when you lead from your values.

Not from fear.
Not from pressure.
Not from the 'way it's always been done.'

But from that place inside you that knows what's right – even when it's hard.

Because when you know what you stand for, your team knows where they stand too.

And that's the essence of psychological safety.

So don't outsource your values to a corporate poster.

Own them. Live them. Lead from them.

That's the kind of leader your team deserves.

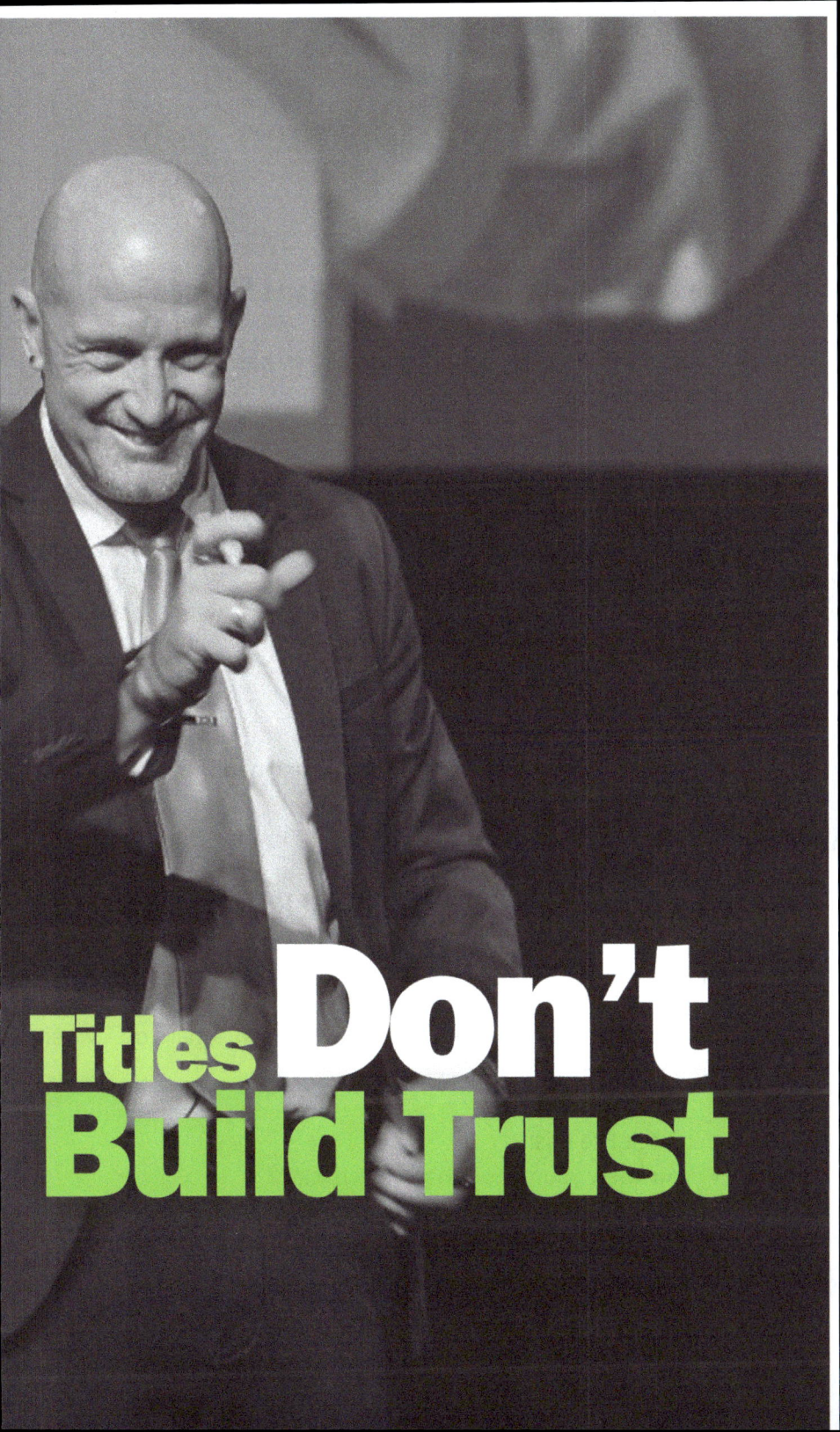

Titles Don't Build Trust

CHAPTER 8: EARNING TRUST AND RESPECT

The Foundations You Can't Fake (and Shouldn't Try To)

If you strip leadership back to its most basic form, you're left with two things:

Trust and respect.

They're not perks. They're not performance bonuses.
They're not conditional on how well your team performs or how loyal they are.

They're the oxygen of high-functioning teams. And psychological safety cannot exist without them.

In this chapter, we'll explore how to build, protect and repair trust and respect – and how to recognise when they're missing.

Because without them? Everything falls apart.

What It Feels Like When Trust and Respect Are Present

Let's flip the lens for a moment.

Think about the best team you've ever been a part of – where you felt valued, safe, and seen.

I bet it felt like this:
- You knew your leader had your back.
- You didn't panic when you made a mistake.
- You could push back on ideas without being punished.
- You were treated like a grown-up, not a problem to manage.

That feeling?

Respect and Trust are pivotal

Psychological safety, as **Amy Edmondson** notes, exists when people feel *interpersonally safe* – free from fear of rejection, ridicule, or resentment.

But trust is the precondition.

Respect is the belief that I matter and that my voice counts.

Trust is the belief that you will act in my best interest. That you will not use what I tell you against me or for the wrong reason.

When either one is absent, fear takes over.

Respecting the Role – but Not the Person

Here's something I've seen play out time and time again:
A team respects the position their leader holds – but they don't trust the person behind it.

They follow directions.
They show up to meetings.
They deliver results.

But behind the scenes?
They don't speak up.
They don't share ideas.
They don't raise concerns.

Why?

Because the leader has authority – but not *authenticity*.

In other words, the team says:
'We'll do what we have to … but we're not bringing our full selves to the table.'

This kind of surface-level compliance might look like performance – but it's not engagement. It's survival.

Titles Don't Build Trust

It's easy to assume respect comes with the title.
And yes, there is a baseline of positional respect that comes with leadership – especially in hierarchical or traditional workplaces.

But here's the hard truth:
Respect for the role does not guarantee trust in the person.

Trust is personal. It's built in small moments of:
- Keeping your word
- Owning your mistakes
- Listening without judgment

Treating people with dignity – *regardless of rank*

Without those behaviours, the role may still be respected. But you won't be followed. Not fully. Not when it counts.

What to Do About It

If you sense your team is following out of duty – not trust – don't panic.

Start rebuilding.

Ask yourself:
- Do I invite challenge, or avoid it?
- Do I listen deeply – or just long enough to reply?
- Do I model the behaviours I expect from others?

Then say this out loud:
'I don't want respect just for the role – I want to earn it through how I show up for you.'

That sentence alone can start the reset.

Timothy R. Clark in *The 4 Stages of Psychological Safety* highlights that contributor safety and challenger safety only happen once trust and respect have been established.

If people don't trust you, they won't speak up.
If people don't feel respected, they won't show up fully.

And the scary part?

Trust takes time to build.
But it can be broken in a single sentence.

Trust, Respect and High Performance

In *Uplift Your Teams,* I explore what really drives sustainable performance – and the answer isn't fear, pressure or blind compliance. It's **trust. Respect. Consistency.** The very things we're talking about in this chapter.

High-performing teams aren't just good at what they do. They're **good at being a team.** And that starts with leaders who create safe environments where people feel:
- Trusted to do the work
- Respected for their perspective
- Empowered to contribute without fear

If those conditions aren't in place, you don't get engagement – you get compliance. And compliance under pressure quickly turns into burnout, turnover or silent disengagement.

In Uplift Your Teams, I lay out the link between **emotional culture and business outcomes** – because performance without psychological safety isn't sustainable. It's a ticking clock.

And if you want your team to last – and thrive – it starts by **uplifting the humans who drive your results.**

Coaching Snapshot: The Thank-You Card That Said Everything

In a coaching session, I met with a leader named *Jenny* who had a thank-you card sitting proudly on her desk.

I asked about it.

'It's from one of my direct reports,' she said. 'He gave it to me after a really tough time at work.'

Inside it read:
'Thanks for having my back when it mattered. I'll never forget it.'

I asked what happened.

'He made a mistake. A big one. I backed him in. Didn't sugarcoat it. Didn't throw him under the bus. We fixed it together. And I made sure everyone knew I still trusted him.'

That's how you enable trust.

You don't earn it with slogans.
You earn it when it's hardest to give.

What Trust and Respect Actually Look Like in Practice

Let's break this down into visible, actionable leadership behaviours.

Building Trust
You build trust when you:
- Follow through on what you say
- Admit when you're wrong
- Protect people's reputations in tough conversations
- Be transparent about what you know – and what you don't
- Give space instead of micromanaging

It's not about being perfect. It's about being *predictable and accountable*.

Showing Respect

You demonstrate respect when you:
- Listen fully, without preparing your rebuttal
- Acknowledge contributions, even if they're small
- Ask before assuming
- Speak to people like adults – not like they owe you something
- Protect dignity in feedback conversations

Respect is not just about manners.
It's about *recognising value* – especially in those who think, act or speak differently from you.

Red Flags: When Trust or Respect Is Missing

You can feel it before you see it. But here are some signs you've got a trust/respect issue on your hands:
- People only say what they think you want to hear.
- Feedback is sugar-coated or non-existent.
- Decisions are made behind closed doors.
- Performance is low, but no one will tell you why.
- Team members don't challenge or stretch each other – they avoid conflict altogether.

Left unchecked, this becomes a culture of **surface agreement and silent disengagement.**

How to Rebuild What's Been Broken

It happens. You make a call that shakes trust. You say something dismissive in a moment of stress. You break someone's confidence.

The question isn't whether you'll mess it up.
The question is: *Will you repair it?*

Here's the process I teach in coaching:

1. Acknowledge it.
'I realise I broke your trust when I [name the behaviour].'

2. Own it.
'That was my decision, and I take full responsibility.'

3. Listen.
Let them speak – even if it's hard to hear.

4. Ask for the reset.
'What would it take for us to rebuild that trust?'

5. Follow through – consistently.
Rebuilding takes actions *repeated over time.*

Real-World Dialogue Templates

After a breach of trust:

'I missed the mark, and I know that impacted you. I want to understand the impact and work on rebuilding your trust.'

To show ongoing respect:

'Your contribution really shaped that outcome – thank you.'

When asking for feedback:

'I want you to be honest with me, even if it's uncomfortable. Your perspective matters.'

To reinforce safety:

'We don't have to agree, but I always want you to feel safe to say it.'

LEADER REFLECTION AND ACTIVITIES

Activity 1: Trust Audit

Reflect on these statements. Rate yourself 1–5
(1 = never, 5 = always):

- I follow through on my promises.
- I own my mistakes without excuses.
- I protect others' dignity, even under pressure.
- I ask for feedback regularly – and mean it.
- I show up predictably, not reactively.

Total

Total your score. Anything below 20? You've got work to do. (And that's okay.)

Activity 2: Respect Mapping

Choose three team members you interact with regularly.
For each, answer:

> *When did I last acknowledge their work?*

> *Have I ever cut them off, dismissed them, or taken credit?*

> *What's one way I can show more respect this week?*

Activity 3: The Rebuild Conversation

Think of someone whose trust you've lost – or whose respect you
may have shaken.

> *Write their name here:* _____
>
> *Now write your opening line for a reset conversation:*
> ,
> _____
> _____ ,

Now schedule it. Don't wait.

COACH'S WRAP-UP

You don't inherit trust – you earn it.

And you don't get respect just because you have a title – you show it first.

If psychological safety is the house we're building, then trust is the foundation, and respect is the front door.

When people trust you:
- They'll tell you the truth.
- They'll take smart risks.
- They'll grow under your leadership.

When they feel respected:
- They'll speak up with ideas.
- They'll care about the outcome.
- They'll treat others the same way.

It's not complicated. But it is sacred.

So ask yourself every day:

'What did I do to build trust today?'
'What did I do to show respect today?'

Then do more of that.

If you don't have *integrity* none of it matters

CHAPTER 9: LIVING WITH INTEGRITY

Leadership That's Real, Reliable and Remembered

Let's strip it all back.

Forget leadership frameworks.
Forget job titles.
Forget strategic plans.

If you don't have integrity – *none of it matters.*

Because leadership without integrity is like a safety harness with a frayed rope.
It might look the part, but when pressure hits? It snaps.

And you can't fake your way out of it.

This chapter is about becoming the kind of leader your team knows they can trust – not just when things are smooth, but when the storm hits.

Because at the core of every psychologically safe team …
Is a leader who keeps their word, lives their values and *doesn't flinch* when it's hard.

What Integrity Actually Means

Let's be clear: integrity isn't about being perfect.

It's not about never making mistakes, or never being challenged.
Integrity is about *alignment.*

Alignment between your values, your words and your behaviour.

You say what you mean.
You do what you say.
And when you mess it up (because you will), you *own it.*

Integrity is quiet. It doesn't show off.
But it is *deeply noticed* – especially by your team.

Coaching Snapshot: 'That's My Thing'

In a coaching program I ran for a utilities company, I met a supervisor named Dean.

He wasn't flashy. He didn't have a huge presence. But his team trusted him – deeply.

I asked one of his crew members what made Dean different.

He said:
'He always follows up. He says he will – and then he does. That's his thing.'

That phrase stuck with me.
'That's his thing.'

Because when a leader is consistent with their words and actions, their team builds a profile of them:
- 'You can count on her.'
- 'He'll tell you the truth.'
- 'She means it when she says it.'

That's what integrity builds.
Reputation. Safety. Loyalty.

Integrity and Psychological Safety

In her research, **Amy Edmondson** doesn't just talk about team openness – she talks about leader credibility. And **credibility starts with integrity.**

If you promise safety, but punish honesty – you lose integrity.
If you talk about wellbeing, but reward overwork – you lose integrity.

If you say 'we're a team,' but play favourites – you lose integrity.

And once it's lost, trust doesn't just dissolve.
It curdles into cynicism.

Timothy R. Clark teaches that psychological safety requires both permission and *protection*.
Integrity provides both.

It gives your team permission to bring their full selves. And it protects them from double standards.

What Integrity Gaps Look Like in the Real World

Integrity gaps aren't always loud. Often, they show up subtly:
- Leaders say 'my door is always open,' but never actually make time.
- They preach feedback, but shut down anything that feels uncomfortable.
- They commit to inclusive practices, but meetings are still dominated by the same two voices.
- They advocate for psychological safety, but joke about 'toughening up.'

You might *mean well.* But if your actions don't match your words, your team is watching – and learning.

They learn:
'It's safer to stay quiet.'
'I can't rely on what they say.'
'This place talks the talk, but doesn't walk it.'

And slowly ... they disengage.

Living with Integrity: Daily Leadership Habits

Here's the good news: integrity isn't a one-time achievement.
It's a *daily decision.*

Let's break down what it looks like in action.

1. Say Less, Mean More
Don't overcommit. Don't promise what you can't deliver.

It's better to say:
'I'll get back to you by Friday,' and do it –
Than to say, 'I'll handle it today,' and forget.

2. Create a Personal Follow-Through System
Use reminders. Calendar blocks. Task apps.

Don't rely on memory for things that matter to others.

Because every time you don't follow through, it sends a message:
'Your need wasn't important enough.'

3. Acknowledge Your Gaps
When you drop the ball, own it.

Try:
'I said I'd follow up, and I didn't. I'm sorry – that's not okay. Here's what I'm doing about it.'

Owning mistakes builds more trust than pretending they didn't happen.

4. Align Your Culture With Your Conduct
Do your behaviours model the culture you say you want?

If not – start with yourself.

Ask:
'Would I want to work for me today?'
That question alone can recalibrate a lot.

Real Talk: Integrity Is Tested When It's Inconvenient

It's easy to lead with integrity when it's smooth sailing.

The real test?

When it costs you.

- When speaking up could upset your boss.
- When backing a team member might make you look weak.
- When pushing back on poor behaviour might spark conflict.

That's when you find out what you really stand for.

And every time you pass that test – even in a small way – your team sees it.

And they think:

'If they can do it, maybe I can too.'

And *that* ... is psychological safety in motion.

And *that* ... is leadership with the right mindset in motion.

Leading with the Right Mindset

One of the biggest lessons I've learned in leadership – and life – is this:

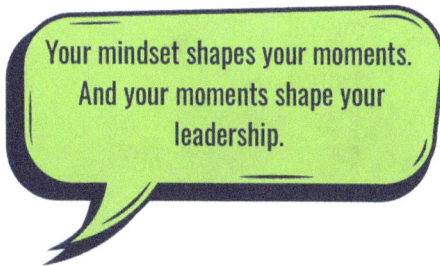

> Your mindset shapes your moments. And your moments shape your leadership.

In my book *Upgrade Your Mindset: How to Be a High-Performance Human*, I explore how our internal thought patterns drive our external behaviours – especially when pressure hits. The same applies to psychological safety.

If your mindset says:

- 'I'm the boss; I need to be right,' you'll resist feedback.
- 'I don't have time to explain,' you'll shut down conversations.
- 'Mistakes are weakness,' you'll lead with blame instead of learning.

But if your mindset says:

- 'Everyone here is doing their best,' you'll stay curious.
- 'My energy sets the tone,' you'll ground yourself before you lead others.
- 'Integrity means aligning my values, words, and actions,' you'll show up consistently – even when it's uncomfortable.

Upgrade Your Mindset is about leading yourself first, so you can lead others better. And when it comes to psychological safety, your mindset isn't just part of the work – it's the foundation of it.

LEADER PRACTICE & ACTIVITIES

Activity 1: The Integrity Mirror

Take 10 quiet minutes and ask:

- Where am I out of alignment right now?
- What am I saying – but not doing?
- What's one small integrity repair I can make this week?

Activity 2: Set a Follow-Through Ritual

Choose a simple ritual to keep your promises visible. For example:

- A Friday 'promise review' calendar reminder.
- A personal whiteboard or digital tracker.
- Asking your EA or team to hold you accountable on specific items.

Write it down:

My ritual will be:

Activity 3: Team Culture Alignment
Ask your team:
'What's one thing we say we value – but don't always act on?'

Document the answer. Share your reflections. Make one change to align closer with that value.

Then say:
'This is part of me working to lead with integrity.'

COACH'S WRAP-UP

Integrity isn't about image. It's about identity.

Who are you when no one's watching?
Who are you when the pressure's on?
Who are you when it would be easier to look away?

The leader with integrity:
- Builds safety.
- Earns trust.
- Sets culture.

And most importantly – sleeps well at night.

So do the work. Live the values. Keep your word.
And when you fall short? Get back up, say the words and *do better.*

That's leadership people will remember. And respect.

SECTION 4:

EMPATHY

EMPATHY

Empathy is not weakness.
It's not softness.
And it's definitely not 'being too emotional'.

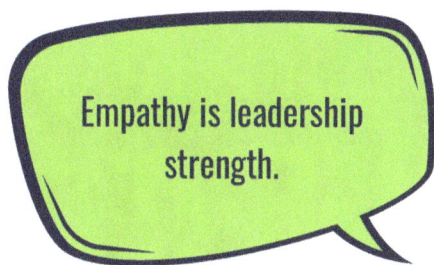

> Empathy is leadership strength.

It's the ability to see the world through someone else's lens.

To understand what might be behind the reaction, the silence, the resistance.

To connect before correcting.

This section is about stepping into the shoes of the people you lead.

Because when people feel understood, they feel safe.

And when they feel safe, they speak. They stretch. They grow.

So let's dive into Chapter 10.

LEADERSHIP THAT

CONNECTS
CALMS
AND CARES

CHAPTER 10: UNDERSTANDING PERSPECTIVES

Leadership That Connects, Calms, and Cares

In Dare to Lead, Brené Brown reminds us that empathy is not about fixing – it's about feeling with. When leaders connect through presence, calm through groundedness, and care through curiosity, they create spaces where people feel seen and safe.

Brown writes, 'Connection is why we're here' – and in leadership, that connection starts with listening, not solving.

True leadership isn't loud; it's attuned, compassionate, and courageous enough to sit with discomfort instead of avoiding it.

How to See What Your Team Sees – Before You Judge or React

Let me say something that might surprise you:

Most of your team's 'bad behaviour' isn't actually about you.

That eye roll?
That resistance to change?
That silence in the meeting?

It might not be disrespect.
It might be fatigue. Frustration. Fear. Misunderstanding.
Or it might be a result of *how they're experiencing the world – right now.*

As a leader, you don't need to agree with everyone. But you must try to understand them.

Because the moment you dismiss someone's experience as invalid, you lose your chance to influence it.

The Team Conflict That Wasn't What It Seemed

Let me take you into a fictionalised real-world example.

I was coaching two senior leaders – Alicia and Tom – locked in tension.
Everything was becoming personal.
Meetings were tense. Emails had a passive-aggressive tone.
And their team? Walking on eggshells.

I brought them into a joint session and said:
'I want each of you to write down what you think the other person is worried about. Then read it back.'

Alicia wrote:
'Tom's worried I'm undermining him in front of his team.'

Tom wrote:
'Alicia's frustrated because I'm not updating her in time.'

Both were right.
Neither had *said* those things.

And once they saw the other person's perspective, empathy entered the room.
They didn't become best mates.
But they started listening again.

That's the power of understanding perspectives.

The Psychology of Perspective-Taking

According to neuroscience research, perspective-taking is a core component of emotional intelligence. It activates parts of the brain responsible for:

- Emotional regulation
- Compassion
- Conflict resolution
- Problem-solving

Amy Edmondson's psychological safety model also references the leader's ability to create *inclusion* by acknowledging and validating different views.

'I see it differently' should not be a threat – it should be an invitation to dialogue.

Timothy R. Clark encourages leaders to lead with empathetic curiosity – especially when confronted with dissent or discomfort.

What Perspective-Shifting Sounds Like

Here are some simple phrases that unlock connection instead of triggering defensiveness:

- 'Help me understand where you're coming from.'
- 'What's your read on this situation?'
- 'What am I missing from your point of view?'
- 'What's it been like for you working through this?'
- 'How are you seeing this play out on your end?'

Then pause.
Let them speak.
Really listen.

This isn't about giving up your position – it's about opening your lens.

Why Leaders Resist Perspective-Taking

It's not that leaders don't care.
But under pressure, most leaders default to efficiency over empathy.

They think:
- 'I don't have time to talk about feelings.'
- 'I know what's going on – why belabour it?'
- 'They're overreacting.'

Here's the trap:
When you dismiss someone's perspective, you don't just silence them – you *shame* them.

And shame is the enemy of safety.

Practical Ways to Build Perspective-Taking into Your Leadership

1. Ask 'What else could be true?'
When someone pushes back or shuts down, ask yourself:
'Besides resistance or laziness, what else might be driving this?'

Maybe it's fear of change.
Maybe it's a value clash.
Maybe it's past trauma around leadership abuse.

You don't need to diagnose it. You just need to consider it.

2. Use the 'Ladder of Inference'
Before reacting, pause and ask:
- What did I observe?
- What story am I telling myself?
- What assumption am I making?
- Could there be another explanation?

This one tool alone can prevent 90% of leadership misunderstandings.

3. De-escalate with 'Tell me more'

Instead of jumping into correction or control, say:
'Tell me more about what's going on for you here.'

Those four words are leadership gold.

Coaching Insight: Curiosity Beats Certainty

In one leadership session, I worked with a manager named Joel who said:
'I'm not a "touchy-feely" guy. I don't get why I need to ask about feelings.'

So I reframed it.

'Joel,' I said, 'You're in charge of performance, right? And performance comes from people, yes?'

He nodded.

"Then your job isn't to be soft. It's to be smart.
And smart leaders ask: *What's driving this behaviour?*"

Empathy isn't softness.

It's *strategic insight.*

It's understanding.

The Next Conversation Isn't About Winning – It's About Understanding

One of the biggest mistakes we make in leadership conversations – especially the uncomfortable ones – is trying to *win.*

We want to be right.
We want to be understood.
We want to move the conversation forward – on our terms.

But in his book The Next Conversation, attorney and communication expert **Jefferson Fisher** reframes that approach entirely.

'You're not trying to win the current conversation,' he writes. 'You're trying to earn the next one.'

That idea is simple. But it's powerful.

Because when emotions run high – whether it's in a feedback loop, a disagreement, or a misalignment in values – the real leadership move is to de-escalate, not dominate.

Fisher outlines that, in your next conversation, your goal should be to:

- Stay emotionally regulated when conversations get heated
- Disarm defensiveness with simple phrases like 'you're not wrong' or 'tell me more'
- Use curiosity instead of control
- Validate the other person without abandoning your point
- Prioritise the relationship over the rebuttal

It's not about giving in. It's about staying in the conversation – so the person you're speaking with doesn't shut down or walk away.

This is especially important in psychologically safe teams.
Because safety is built not when we agree – but when we feel heard.

Fisher challenges us to stop treating conversations as battles and start treating them as bridges. The goal isn't to be right. The goal is to stay connected – even in the discomfort.

And that requires one of the greatest leadership skills of all: **empathy under pressure.**

So the next time you feel like saying, *'Why don't they get it?'*
Ask instead: *'What haven't I heard yet?'*

That's where your next breakthrough conversation begins.

LEADER REFLECTION AND ACTIVITIES

Activity 1: The Perspective Swap
Think of a team member who frustrates you.
Write down:

Their Name:

What behaviour frustrates you?

What's the story you're telling yourself about them?

Now: What else could be true about why they behave this way?

Activity 2: 'Tell Me More' Week

This week, commit to using the phrase 'Tell me more …' at least once per day – especially when tempted to correct or dismiss. Reflect:

What did I learn?

What surprised me?

How did it shift the conversation?

Activity 3: Team Empathy Round

In your next meeting, ask:

'What's something people might not realise about what it's like to do your role?'

You'll be amazed what emerges.

And so will your team.

COACH'S WRAP-UP

You don't have to agree with someone to understand them.

You just have to care enough to try.

And when you do?

You:
- Defuse conflict.
- Build connection.
- Create safety.

Empathy doesn't mean giving up your view.

It means giving room for theirs.

And when people feel seen, they show up differently. They engage. They grow.

So the next time you're tempted to say, 'They just don't get it,' – pause.

Ask instead: 'What don't I get yet?'

That's where real leadership begins.

Mindfulness

IS CHOOSING HOW YOU

Lead

EVEN WHEN THE
HEAT IS ON

CHAPTER 11: MINDFULNESS FOR STRESS MANAGEMENT

How to Stay Present, Respond (Not React) and Lead with Calm

Let me paint a picture.

You've got back-to-back meetings.

Your inbox is overflowing.

A supplier just dropped the ball.

And a team member's standing in your doorway with 'a quick question' – the kind that isn't quick at all.

In that moment, what happens next defines your leadership.

Will you react?

Or will you respond?

That's where mindfulness comes in.

Because mindfulness isn't about meditation cushions and incense.

It's about *presence.*

It's about control.

It's about choosing how you lead – even when the heat is on.

This chapter is your practical guide to leading with more breath, less burnout.

What Is Mindfulness (Really)?

Mindfulness is simply the ability to:
- Be aware of what's happening right now
- Without judgment
- And with intentional attention

It's the skill of noticing:
- 'I'm clenching my jaw.'
- 'I'm about to say something I'll regret.'
- 'I'm spiralling into worst-case scenarios.'

And instead of reacting on autopilot, you pause. You breathe. You choose.
That's powerful leadership.

As **Daniel Goleman** (author of Emotional Intelligence) puts it:
'Mindfulness gives you the space between stimulus and response.'

And in that space?
Leadership lives.

Leadership Under Pressure: The BOOM Moment

I've talked about BOOM moments in other chapters – the moments when things go sideways.

In a BOOM moment, your nervous system goes into fight-flight-freeze mode.
Your thinking brain takes a back seat.
Your emotional brain grabs the wheel.

You feel it:
- Heart racing
- Breathing shallow
- Tunnel vision
- Snappy words

- Regret, seconds later

Mindfulness helps you *interrupt* that pattern.

Instead of reacting with emotion, you respond with intention.

You create what I call **conscious control.**

Real-Life Coaching Story: The Mindful Breather

Let me tell you about Caleb, a shift leader I coached in a high-pressure plant environment.

Smart guy. Well-liked. But he had a temper under stress.

He came to me after snapping at a technician in front of the whole crew. 'I lost it,' he said. 'And I hate that I did.'

We worked on a *30-second breathing ritual* before toolbox talks:
- One slow breath in through the nose
- Hold for four counts
- Exhale slowly through the mouth
- Repeat twice
- Ground feet on the floor
- Speak

Within two weeks, his entire team noticed a difference.

They said:
'You seem calmer.'
'It's like you're more present.'
'You actually listen now.'

All from two mindful breaths.

What the Research Says

Studies from Harvard, Stanford, and the Centre for Mindful Leadership show that mindfulness:

- Lowers cortisol (the stress hormone)
- Increases executive function (decision-making)
- Boosts empathy and listening
- Improves memory and focus

Amy Edmondson notes that psychological safety requires leaders to 'model calm,' especially during uncertainty.

And **Timothy R. Clark** reminds us that 'emotional regulation is the first form of self-leadership.'

Mindfulness gives you that.

Mindfulness Practices for Busy Leaders

You don't need to sit cross-legged for an hour to benefit from mindfulness.

Here are tools you can build into your leadership day:

1. The 3-Breath Reset
Anytime you feel triggered, overwhelmed, or agitated:
- Stop.
- Take three slow, deep breaths.
- With each exhale, say to yourself: 'Let go.'

2. The 60-Second Pause Before a Meeting
Before you lead a meeting, ask yourself:
'How do I want to show up right now?'
Then breathe for 60 seconds – no agenda, just presence.

3. The Daily Debrief
At the end of each day, ask:
- 'What went well?'
- 'What triggered me?'
- 'How did I respond?'

This builds self-awareness over time – and shows you where to grow.

4. Mindful Listening

In your next 1-on-1, give the other person your full attention.
No phone. No multitasking. No jumping in to solve.
Just listen. Fully.

Your presence is your power.

Real-World Application: Leading While Grounded

I once coached a senior leader, Melissa, during an organisational restructure.

It was chaos. People were anxious. Emotions were high.

She made a commitment: to start every leadership call with 60 seconds of silent breathing.

At first, people were sceptical. But within a week, they requested it.

Her team said:
'It helps us focus.'
'We feel calmer, clearer, more present.'

That's leadership. Not adding noise – creating space.

Common Mindfulness Myths (And Why They're Wrong)

'I don't have time.'
You don't have time not to. Even 1 minute counts.

'It's just woo-woo.'
Neuroscience says otherwise. It's biology, not Buddhism.

'I'm bad at it.'
There's no "bad" at mindfulness – only practice.

LEADER REFLECTION AND ACTIVITIES

Activity 1: Your Mindful Moment

Choose a time each day to pause for 60 seconds and breathe. Set a reminder. Make it a ritual.

Write

- *My pause time: _____*

- *My prompt phrase: _____*
  (e.g., 'Let go', 'Show up', 'Breathe'.)

Activity 2: Reaction Reflection

Think of a moment this week when you reacted instead of responded.

- What triggered it?
- How did it feel?
- What could you do differently next time?

Write your mindful response plan below.

Activity 3: Try the Meeting Reset

Before your next team meeting, invite the group to take 30 seconds of silent breath. Then ask:

'What would help us be fully present right now?'

Debrief the impact afterward. Capture the feedback.

COACH'S WRAP-UP

Here's the truth: leadership will always be stressful.

But how you meet that stress is up to you.

Mindfulness gives you:
- Presence over panic
- Response over reaction
- Grace under fire

And in doing so, it gives your team something else:

A leader who's grounded.

A leader who models safety.

A leader they can breathe around.

So take the pause.

Take the breath.

Take the moment to check in – before you speak out.

That's leadership that lasts.

You don't need
TO WIN
EVERY CONFLICT
STAY CALM
CLEAR
AND
CONGRUENT
WITH YOUR VALUES

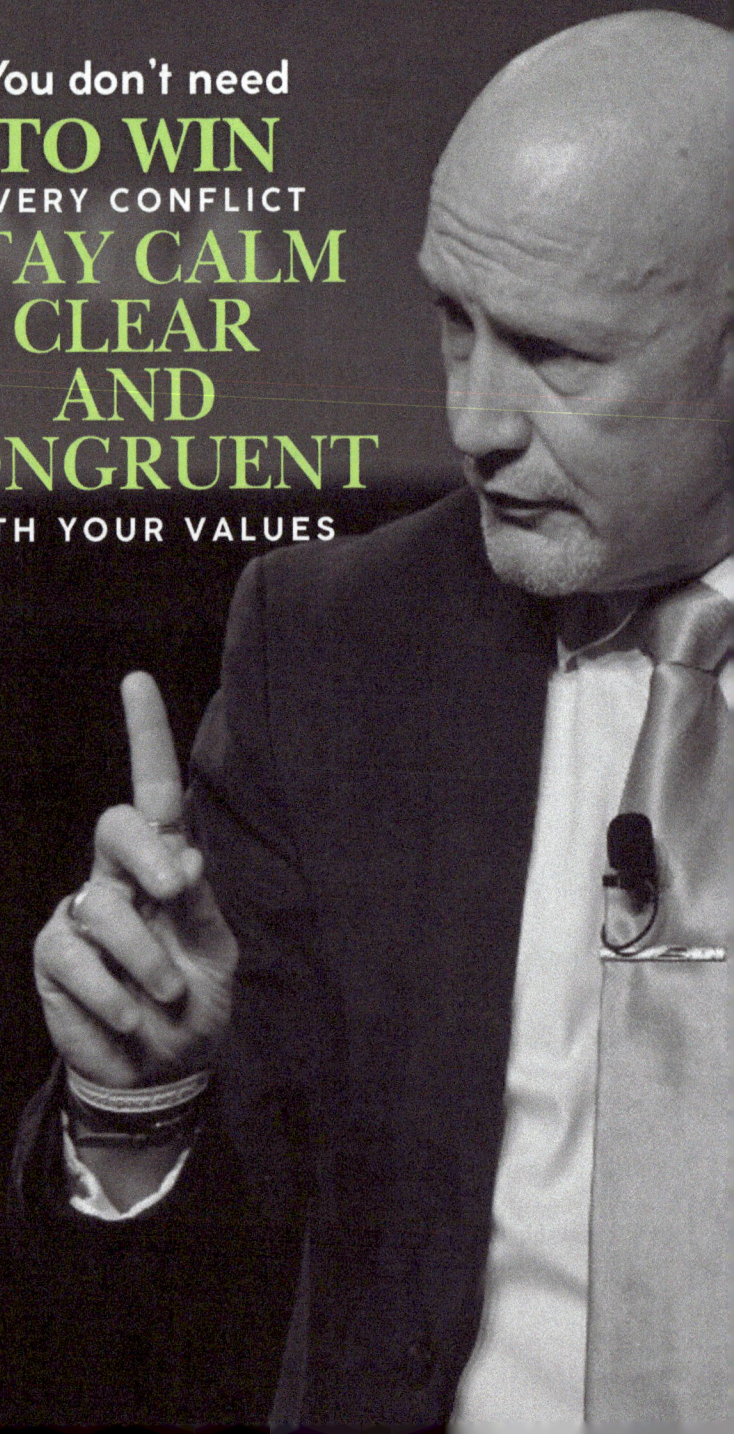

CHAPTER 12: DEALING WITH DIFFICULT COLLEAGUES

How to Hold Space, Set Boundaries and Stay Professional Under Pressure

Let's talk about the real stuff.

The stuff leaders whisper to coaches behind closed doors:

'I've got someone on the team who's just … *difficult.*'
'They're defensive. Negative. *Uncooperative.*'
'I've tried everything, *but nothing works.*'
'It's draining. It's exhausting. *And I'm losing sleep over it.*'

Sound familiar?

You're not alone.
Every leader no matter how skilled, experienced, or emotionally intelligent – eventually hits a wall with someone who just pushes their buttons.

But here's the truth:

Difficult colleagues aren't always bad people.
And handling them well doesn't mean tolerating bad behaviour.

This chapter will help you walk that fine line between empathy and accountability.

Because psychological safety doesn't mean avoiding hard conversations.

It means having them – with care, clarity and courage.

Why Some People Feel 'Difficult'

Let's reframe the word for a second.

When someone's behaviour feels difficult, it's often because:

- It *conflicts* *with your values*
- It *disrupts* *your flow*
- It *activates* *your emotional history* (yes, that stuff matters)
- It *exposes* *a gap in trust or clarity*

And sometimes, it's not even about them – it's about what they represent.

A team member who resists change might remind you of a parent who always shut you down.

A peer who talks over you might trigger memories of never being heard in meetings.

The person isn't always the *problem.*
Sometimes, they're just the *mirror.*

Coaching Snapshot: The Chronic Interrupter

Let me share a fictionalised version of a true coaching moment.

A senior leader I was working with – *Tanya* – had a peer who constantly interrupted her during cross-functional meetings.

At first, she brushed it off.

Then she started to withdraw. She contributed less. Her confidence took a hit.

She said:
'I feel like I'm being erased in real time.'

We developed a short, respectful line she could use in the moment:
'Can I finish that thought before we move on?'

It worked.

The interrupter backed off. Others took the cue. Tanya reclaimed her space.

The relationship didn't become perfect – but it became professional again.

That's leadership in action.

How to Navigate Difficult Dynamics (Without Losing It)

Here's a practical framework I teach in every leadership coaching program. It's called the CARE Model:

C – Clarify the Behaviour

What's actually happening? Describe it like a CCTV camera would.

'They're toxic.'
'They cut off others mid-sentence. They sigh loudly when people speak. They ignore agreed deadlines.'

This reduces emotional heat and helps you respond *with data, not drama.*

A – Acknowledge the Impact

What effect is the behaviour having on you, the team, or the work?

'When you speak over people, I notice the rest of the team shuts down.'
'When you miss deadlines, it puts pressure on the rest of us.'

Keep it about the behaviour, not the person.

R – Request a Change

Be specific. Be respectful. Be firm.

'Can I ask that we give each speaker time to finish before responding?'

'Going forward, I need you to update the tracker by 3PM each Friday.'

Clear is kind.

E – Empathise and Explore

Give them a chance to share their side. There might be more going on.

'Is there something that's been making this difficult for you lately?'
'What would make it easier to follow through on that next time?'

Empathy doesn't excuse bad behaviour.
It helps you understand it – and solve it together.

When Behaviour Crosses the Line

Let's be clear: psychological safety does not mean tolerating:
- Bullying
- Harassment
- Discrimination
- Gaslighting
- Aggression
- Repeated boundary violations

If a colleague's behaviour consistently causes harm or fear, you have a responsibility to:
- Document it
- Address it directly (if safe to do so)
- Escalate through appropriate channels
- Protect yourself and your team

This isn't just a leadership issue – it's a legal one.

Mindsets That Help You Stay Grounded

These mental reframes have helped dozens of leaders I've coached:

- 'They're not *difficult.* They're *human* – and possibly in pain.'
- 'Their behaviour is *about them*, not about me.'
- 'I can hold boundaries and be kind.'
- 'I can lead the tone of this interaction, even if I can't control the outcome.'

Remember: you don't need to win every conflict.
You just need to stay calm, clear and congruent with your values.

LEADER REFLECTION AND ACTIVITIES

Activity 1: The CARE Model in Action
Think of a challenging dynamic you're currently facing. Write it below.

Person: _____
What's the observable behaviour?

What's the impact?

What request will you make?

What will you ask or explore with empathy?

Activity 2: Your Reaction Reflection

What triggers you most in this person's behaviour?

What might be underneath that trigger (for them or for you)?

How can you ground yourself before your next interaction?

Activity 3: Boundaries Reset

Write down 1–2 boundaries you need to reinforce or re-establish with a colleague.

Boundary:

How will you communicate it clearly and respectfully?

When will you have the conversation?

Commit to the conversation this week. Don't delay. You'll feel lighter the moment it's done.

COACH'S WRAP-UP

Difficult colleagues are part of the leadership landscape.

But they don't have to drain your energy or destroy your culture.

Here's the leadership path:
- Understand what's driving the behaviour
- Separate the person from the problem
- Set respectful, clear boundaries
- Stay curious, not combative
- Hold space – but hold the line

Because when you deal with conflict well, you don't just protect psychological safety – you *strengthen* it.

So the next time someone feels 'difficult', pause and ask:

'What does this moment need from me as a leader?'

Then breathe.

Lead.

And do it with empathy *and* strength.

CLOSING: SPEAK SAFE. LEAD BRAVE. STAY HUMAN.

The End Is the Beginning

If you've made it this far, you're not just a reader.

You're a leader who cares.
You care enough to reflect.
You care enough to learn.
You care enough to grow.

And that, in itself, sets you apart.

Because here's the truth: most leaders don't finish books like this.
They start them. They skim them. Then they go back to their inbox.

But you *stayed.*

And that tells me something important:

You're ready to do the work – to lead in a way that creates safety, not silence.

Leadership Isn't Perfect. But It Should Be Personal.

If there's one message I want you to carry forward from this book, it's this:

Psychological safety starts with *you.*

Not with HR policies.
Not with posters.
Not with an annual culture survey.

It starts with the way you speak.
The way you listen.
The way you own your energy in a meeting.

It starts with the *courage to go first* – to model vulnerability, ask better questions, set clearer boundaries, and deal with difficult moments instead of avoiding them.

Leadership isn't about perfection.
It's about *presence.*
About choosing to show up better, again and again.

It's a Cycle. Not a Checkbox.

Building psychological safety is not a one-time fix.
It's not:
- 'We talked about values once.'
- 'We had a good month.'
- 'Nobody's complained lately, so we're fine.'

It's a daily practice. A leadership rhythm.

Every conversation is a chance to build safety – or break it.
Every email. Every meeting. Every moment.

So keep doing the reps.

Because safety, like fitness, is a muscle.
You either use it – or lose it.

Your Leadership Legacy

One day, people will talk about you.

The question is: *What will they say?*
Will they say:
- 'She made me feel smart.'
- 'He backed me when it counted.'

- 'They listened. Properly.'
- 'I never felt afraid to speak up.'

Or will they say:
- 'They were always too busy.'
- 'I never knew where I stood.'
- 'I didn't feel safe.'

You are building your leadership legacy every day.
Word by word. Action by action.

So choose consciously.

Because how people feel around you is the thing they'll remember most.

What to Do Next

You might be wondering – *where do I go from here?*

Here's my suggestion:

✅ **Pick One Chapter**
Go back to the one that hit hardest. Re-read it. Do the activity. Apply it this week.

✅ **Have One Conversation**
Whether it's a values convo, a feedback loop, or a difficult reset – start the dialogue.

✅ **Set One Safety Goal**
What's one thing you'll do to lift safety in your team this month?

Write it down. Say it out loud. Share it with someone. Then follow through.

A PERSONAL THANK YOU

From me to you – thank you.

Thank you for caring enough to learn what it really means to lead safe.
Thank you for doing the work that most avoid.
Thank you for being the kind of leader the world needs more of – one who speaks with purpose, leads with empathy and makes work better for everyone around them.

I wrote this book not as a rulebook, but as a *conversation*.

One that sounds like me. One that (I hope) *feels* like you.

Because at the end of the day, leadership is human work.

Messy. Imperfect. Brave.

And so are you.

YOUR FINAL REFLECTION

As you close this book, take a moment.
Grab a pen. Get quiet. And answer these:
- What's one thing this book helped you remember about leadership?
- What's one mindset or message you're going to carry forward?
- What's one thing you'll do differently tomorrow?

And finally:
- What kind of leader do you want to be remembered as?

Write it. Say it. Then live it.

SPEAK SAFE. LEAD BRAVE. STAY HUMAN.

You don't have to lead loudly.
You don't have to lead perfectly.
But you do have to lead from a place that's real.

That's how safety is built.
That's how trust is earned.
That's how legacies are made.

So wherever you go next – go as a leader who speaks safe.

Because the teams you lead … are waiting.

ACTION PLANS FROM EACH CHAPTER

Chapter 1: What You Say Matters

Key message:

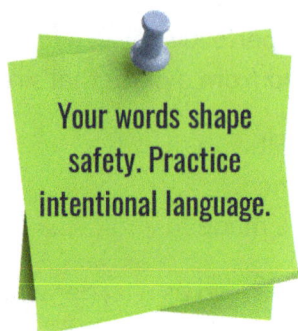

Your words shape
safety. Practice
intentional language.

Try This:

- Replace 'Let's get this over with' with 'Thanks for making the time.'
- Use openers like: 'What's your take on this?'

REFLECTION:

How do your words create (or kill) safety in your team?

Chapter 2: The Drivers of Psychological Safety

Key message:

Safety is built on trust, respect, consistency, and care.

Try This:
- Begin meetings with check-ins.
- Use follow-through to build trust.

REFLECTION:

Which driver is your strength? Which needs more work?

Chapter 3: The Compliance and Legal Aspects of Psychological Safety

Key message:

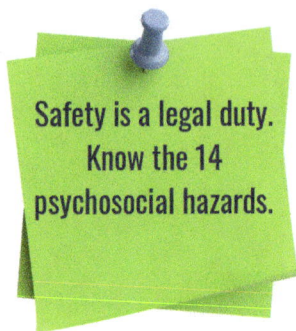

Safety is a legal duty.
Know the 14
psychosocial hazards.

Try This:
- Audit your team against the 14 elements.
- Start a discussion: 'Where might we be at risk?'

REFLECTION:

What's one hazard you've overlooked?

Chapter 4: Everyone Is Different

Key message:

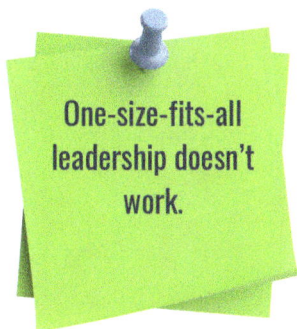

One-size-fits-all leadership doesn't work.

Try This:
- Ask team members how they prefer to receive feedback.
- Learn one new thing about each person's style.

REFLECTION:

Who on your team needs you to adjust your approach?

Chapter 5: All Voices Should Be Heard

Key message:

Quiet voices matter.
Make space.

Try This:
- Rotate meeting facilitation.
- Use the prompt: 'Tell me more.'

REFLECTION:

Who's missing from the conversation – and why?

Chapter 6: Boundaries Are Important

Key message:

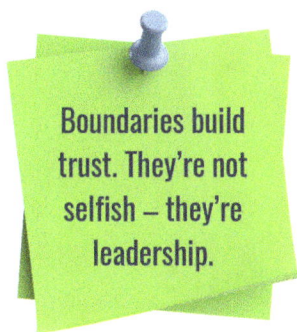

Boundaries build trust. They're not selfish – they're leadership.

Try This:
- Set core hours and protect deep work time.
- Say no to low-value meetings.

REFLECTION:

Where are you saying yes too often?

Chapter 7: Leading from Your Values

Key message:

Leadership grounded
in values builds
safety.

Try This:
- Name your top 3 values.
- Align a difficult decision with those values.

REFLECTION:

Where are you out of alignment right now?

Chapter 8: Earning Trust and Respect

Key message:

Respect is earned.
Trust is built daily.

Try This:
- Show up consistently.
- Acknowledge effort and feedback.

REFLECTION:

When did you last repair a trust slip?

Chapter 9: Living with Integrity

Key message:

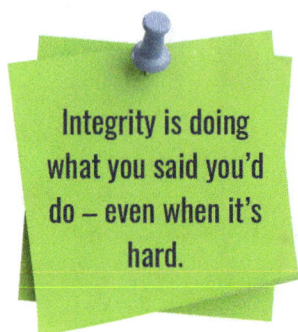

Integrity is doing what you said you'd do – even when it's hard.

Try This:
- Set a weekly review to track follow-through.
- Acknowledge when you miss the mark.

REFLECTION:

What's one commitment you need to honour this week?

Chapter 10: Understanding Perspectives

Key message:

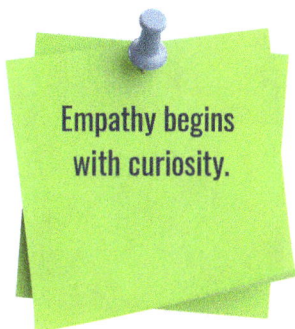

Empathy begins
with curiosity.

Try This:
- Ask: 'What might be true for them?'
- Run a team empathy exercise.

REFLECTION:

Who frustrates you – and what else could be true about them?

Chapter 11: Mindfulness for Stress Management

Key message:

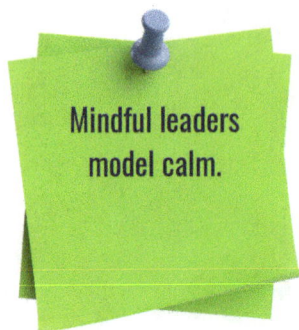

Mindful leaders
model calm.

Try This:
- Pause for 60 seconds before a hard conversation.
- Breathe intentionally.

REFLECTION:

Where could mindfulness improve your reactions?

Chapter 12: Dealing with Difficult Colleagues

Key message:

Lead with boundaries and empathy.

Try This:
- Use the CARE model (Clarify, Acknowledge, Request, Empathise).
- Practice de-escalation language.

REFLECTION:

What conversation are you avoiding – and why?

REFERENCED LEADERSHIP & PSYCHOLOGY BOOKS

1. Dare to Lead: Brave Work. Tough Conversations. Whole Hearts.
   Brené Brown, Random House (2018)
2. Extreme Ownership: How U.S. Navy SEALs Lead and Win
   Jocko Willink and Leif Babin, St. Martin's Press (2015)
3. Let's Talk About Safety: 19 Ways You Can Work Safely
   Anton Guinea, The Guinea Group (2020)
4. Next Generation Safety Leadership: From Compliance to Care
   Clive Lloyd, Safety Futures (2021)
5. Radical Candor: Be a Kick-Ass Boss Without Losing Your Humanity
   Kim Scott, St. Martin's Press (2017)
6. Surrounded by Idiots: The Four Types of Human Behavior and
   How to Effectively Communicate with Each in Business (and in
   Life)
   Thomas Erikson, St. Martin's Essentials (2019)
7. The 4 Stages of Psychological Safety: Defining the Path to
   Inclusion and Innovation
   Timothy R. Clark, Berrett-Koehler Publishers (2020)
8. The Fearless Organization: Creating Psychological Safety in the
   Workplace for Learning, Innovation, and Growth
   Amy C. Edmondson, Wiley (2018)
9. The Next Conversation: Transform Your Uncomfortable
   Conversations Into Breakthroughs
   Jefferson Fisher
   Harper Horizon, 2024
10. The Remix: How to Lead and Succeed in the Multigenerational
    Workplace
    Lindsey Pollak, Harper Business (2019)
11. Upgrade Your Mindset: How to Be a High-Performance Human
    Anton Guinea, The Guinea Group (2021)
12. Uplift Your Teams: The Psychology of Performance and
    Psychological Safety
    Anton Guinea, The Guinea Group (2023)
13. Upskill Your Leadership: Lead Yourself Before You Lead Others
    Anton Guinea, The Guinea Group (2022)

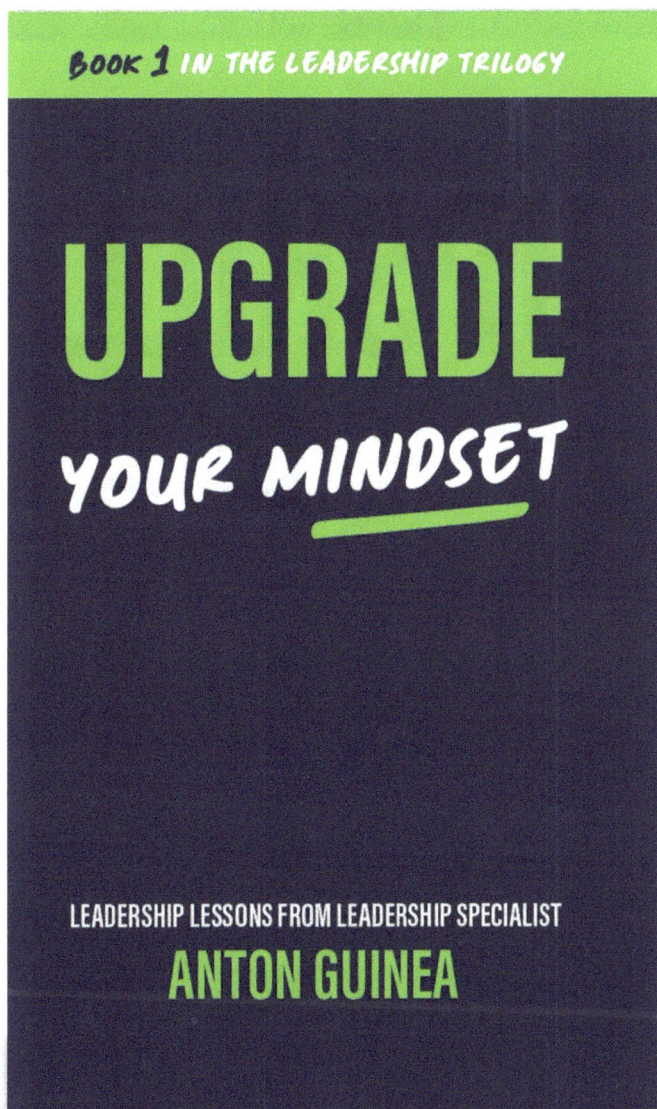

BOOK 1 IN THE LEADERSHIP TRILOGY

UPGRADE
YOUR MINDSET

LEADERSHIP LESSONS FROM LEADERSHIP SPECIALIST
ANTON GUINEA

Available at: Upgrade your Mindset – The Guinea Group

Available at: Upskill Your Leadership – The Guinea Group

Available at: Uplift Your Teams – The Guinea Group

Available at: The Guinea Group
Let's Talk About Safety – eBook
Let's Talk About Safety – Hardcover
Let's Talk About Safety – Audiobook

Conversation Planner

Overview of the conversation

Name .... Date: ....

Location ....

Purpose of the Conversation

Discussion Points

○ ....

○ ....

○ ....

Close out of the conversation (with actions)

Psychosocial Hazard Checklist for Leaders

Use this checklist to identify and address psychosocial risks in your team. Adapted from Safe Work Australia's psychosocial hazard guidelines, these 14 elements are leadership touchpoints that influence psychological safety, wellbeing, and compliance. Each of these risks should be also addressed with an organisational policy and procedure.

Psychosocial Hazard	What to Look For	Out of 10	Your Leadership Action	By
Job Demands	Unreasonable workload, high pressure, burnout signs		Rebalanced workload. Ask: What support do you need?	
Low Job Control	Micromanagement, no autonomy		Delegate decisions. Ask: How would you like to do this?	
Poor Support	No guidance or regular check-ins		Book consistent 1-on-1s. Be visible.	
Lack of Role Clarity	Confused responsibilities, double handling		Clarify roles. Position Descriptions. Use RACI charts.	
Poor Change Management	Late updates, confusion, disengagement		Communicate early—even if incomplete.	
Inadequate Recognition	Effort goes unnoticed, demotivation		Say thank you. Celebrate wins in public and in private.	
Poor Relationships	Cliques, gossip, exclusion		Set team norms. Model respectful dialogue.	
Bullying	Aggression, intimidation, mocking		Zero tolerance. Investigate immediately.	
Harassment	Unwelcome comments, power misuse		Act quickly. Provide clear reporting paths.	
Ongoing Conflict	Frequent tension, unresolved disputes		Facilitate mediation. Teach respectful challenge.	
Remote Isolation	Disconnection, forgotten workers		Schedule connection rituals. Personal check-ins.	
Aggression/Violence	Verbal or physical threats		Enforce safety protocols. Escalate as needed.	
Traumatic Exposure	Work linked to trauma or distress		Offer EAP. Normalise debriefing.	
Poor Conditions	Noise, heat, bad lighting, discomfort		Fix environment. Raise facility requests quickly.	

Speak Safe Self Diagnostic Tool

Use this checklist to identify and address areas that you could improve on as a leader, to increase the psychological safety of your team!

Psychological Safety Element	What to Look For	Out of 10	Your Leadership Action	By
What you say matters	How well and how often do you correct yourself and check your languaging?			
The drivers of psychological safety	How well do you apply the four stages of psychological safety?			
The compliance and legal aspects of Psychological Safety	How well have you implemented the 14 elements of psychological safety?			
Everyone is different	How much do you focus on diversity when making decisions?			
All voices should be heard	How well do you listen to understand, as opposed to listening to reply?			
Boundaries are important	How well do you set personal and team boundaries?			
Leading from your values	How clear are you on your own personal values and are they aligned to the organisational values?			
Earning trust and respect	What level of trust do you put in your team members to do their jobs?			
Living with integrity	At what level do you follow through on commitments that you make to your team?			
Understanding perspectives	How open are you to the views and opinions of others, particularly those different to your own?			
Mindfulness for stress management	How well do you manage your stress levels with mindful techniques?			
Dealing with difficult colleagues	How well do you deal with difficult conversations and difficult colleagues or team members?			

ABOUT THE AUTHOR

20 years of working with leaders and their teams

Anton Guinea is a leadership coach, keynote speaker, behavioural safety specialist – and someone who knows first-hand what it means to face a life-changing moment.

After surviving a near-fatal electrical explosion early in his career, Anton committed his life to making workplaces safer – not just physically, but psychologically. That experience didn't just change his body. It changed his mindset, his mission, and how he saw leadership from the inside out.

With over two decades of experience working with frontline teams, operational leaders, and executive boards across Australia and internationally, Anton brings a rare blend of hard-earned insight and heartfelt delivery to every room he enters. Through his company, The Guinea Group, he has helped thousands of leaders lift their performance, own their impact, and lead with courage – even under pressure.

Anton is the author of five books including Upgrade Your Mindset, Upskill Your Leadership, Uplift Your Teams, Let's Talk About Safety, and now Speak Safe – his most personal and practical work yet.

When he's not working with leaders to build safer, stronger teams, you'll find Anton with his family, on stage inspiring audiences, or challenging the way the world thinks about what leadership should really feel like.

Because safety isn't just compliance – it's culture.

And leadership isn't just a role – it's a responsibility.

TRAINING AND COACHING WITH ANTON AND THE GUINEA GROUP

Take the next step from reading to real-life results

Reading *Speak Safe* is a powerful start – but if you're ready to bring psychological safety to life in your team, workplace, or organisation, we're here to help.

At The Guinea Group, we deliver high-impact, human-focused training and coaching programs that give leaders the tools, language, and mindset to lead safer, stronger teams.

WE WORK WITH:

✔ Frontline supervisors who want to improve communication and culture
✔ Middle managers who need to reset trust and team dynamics
✔ Senior leaders who want to embed psychological safety across the business

OUR CORE PROGRAMS

Speak Safe Leadership Program

Based on the principles in this book, this program teaches leaders how to create safety through communication, empathy, values-driven behaviour, and courageous conversations.

Fearless Public Speaking for Leaders

The Guinea Group's Public Speaking for Leaders program equips leaders with the confidence, clarity, and storytelling skills to speak with impact – whether it's in a boardroom, on a stage, or to their team.

Pressure-Proof Leadership Coaching

One-on-one or small-group coaching for leaders who want to show up better under pressure, reset their mindset, and lead with calm and clarity – even in the tough stuff.

Let's Talk
If you're ready to move from information to transformation, we'd love to hear from you.

📍 Visit: www.theguineagroup.com.au
✉ Email: theteam@theguineagroup.com.au
📞 Call: 0422 058 736

LET'S BUILD SAFER, STRONGER, MORE HUMAN WORKPLACES — TOGETHER.